Home Preserving & Bottling

Gladys Mann

HAMLYN
London New York Sydney Toronto

First published in
the LEISURE-PLAN series in 1970 by
THE HAMLYN PUBLISHING GROUP LIMITED
London New York Sydney Toronto
Astronaut House Feltham Middlesex England
© *Copyright The Hamlyn Publishing Group Limited 1974*
Second edition 1974
ISBN 0 600 34428 2
Printed in England by Chapel River Press Andover Hants

ACKNOWLEDGMENTS
The author and publishers thank the following for
their kind co-operation in
supplying colour photographs for this book
CEREBOS FOODS LTD
Pickled red cabbage page 55
CEREBOS FOODS LTD
distributors of Atora shredded beef suet
Making mincemeat page 31
FRUIT PRODUCERS' COUNCIL
Raspberry jam, Pear and marrow ginger page 51
Pear and apricot jam, Apple and apricot jam,
Apple and fig jam, Apple and cinnamon butter,
Apple and red pepper chutney, Mint sauce page 51
Pear sections in almond syrup page 31
Apple and cucumber pickle,
Sweet spiced apple pieces page 55
Greengage jam, Bramble and apple jelly,
Plum wine, Bottled plums page 63

Jacket photograph by John Lee
Illustrated by Richard Osborne

The black and white photographs are by courtesy of
ANGEL STUDIOS
Dried apple rings page 67
AUSTRALIAN RECIPE SERVICE
Australian sweet chutney page 53
BOOTS THE CHEMIST
Wine making, bottling and corking equipment page 72
BRITISH EGG INFORMATION SERVICE
Spiced eggs page 60
J & J COLMAN LTD
Corn relish making mustard pickle page 44
Norwich apple chutney page 50
Spiced tomato relish page 57
FRUIT PRODUCERS' COUNCIL
Clear mixed pickles page 41
Peppered apple rings page 46
PRESTIGE LTD
Preparing grapefruit marmalade page 24
Bottling vegetables page 37

Contents

Introduction

Living in a time when the food manufacturers put every conceivable commodity into cans, jars, bottles or packets, it is not surprising that home preserving is becoming a lost art. While we spend a great deal of money for the convenience that bought preserved foods provide, we are forgetting the true flavour of home preserved fruits and vegetables. And yet the making of preserves, pickles and chutneys is one of the most satisfying of all branches of cookery; it is interesting and relaxing, and the rewards – all those jars of jam, marmalade and jelly ready for tea, bottled fruits for puddings or pies, the pickles and chutneys to cheer up the cold joint, or to add unusual flavour to stews, curries and casseroles – make the time and trouble taken worthwhile.

However good the manufacturer (and today, many are very good), his products cannot compare for flavour and goodness, with the home-made article. If you have a suitable garden, you can grow plenty of produce, and use the surplus to make your own pickles and preserves at little cost. If you don't have a garden you can buy fruits and berries quite cheaply when there is a glut. Search the country lanes and woods for blackberries, and elderberries – free for the picking; make use of windfall apples and pears, and the homely rhubarb – they make excellent jellies, chutneys and pickles and cost little or nothing. The most expensive jams and bottled fruits are peaches and apricots. At the height of their season they are reasonably cheap and it is worthwhile making some of these luxury preserves. They are just as easy to deal with as the more everyday fruits such as strawberries or plums.

Curing one's own hams is another most rewarding occupation, especially where there is a growing family to cater for, and it is very economical to prepare the Christmas ham oneself. The drying and salting of vegetables and fruits also helps the household budget considerably, and more and more people are realising that it is quite simple to preserve herbs from one's own garden. These can be dried, or stored in the home freezer, as, of course, can any surplus garden produce.

Another old kitchen craft is the home brewing of wines – the last few years have seen a renewed interest and many people have started to make their own; not only country people whose families made wine from roots, flowers, berries and fruits, using recipes handed down for generations, but towns-people who at one time would not look at any wine unless it came from France, Italy or Germany.

There is nothing particularly difficult about wine-making, and while the simplest utensils found in most kitchens can be used, you can have an enthralling time using the special wine-making kits and extras, or additives, supplied by wine-making equipment shops, or one of the larger store chemists.

These wine-making kits and extras are intended to make the process foolproof and, no doubt, will be reassuring to the amateur; but in wine-making, experience is the best teacher of all. Experience and patience, say the old folk, make the best wine. Especially patience; to most people the most difficult part is the long waiting before they can sample the end-product. For no wine is really fit to drink until it is at least twelve months old.

Preserving – caution

Preserving of vegetables by bottling is recommended only when a pressure cooker is used, see page 37.

If there is any doubt about the goodness of bottled vegetables when the jars are opened – if they smell musty or if there is any appearance of mushiness or sliminess – throw them away *without tasting*. All bottled vegetables should be boiled for a minute or two *before* they are tasted, as a safeguard.

Oven Temperatures

Description	Electric Setting	Gas Mark
very cool	225°F – 110°C	¼
	250°F – 130°C	½
cool	275°F – 140°C	1
	300°F – 150°C	2
moderate	325°F – 170°C	3
	350°F – 180°C	4
moderately hot	375°F – 190°C	5
	400°F – 200°C	6
hot	425°F – 220°C	7
	450°F – 230°C	8
very hot	475°F – 240°C	9

Note

This table is an approximate guide only. Different makes of cooker vary and if you are in any doubt about the setting it is as well to refer to the manufacturer's temperature chart.

Making chutney

Jam and Jelly Making

I am so often asked why jam is runny or why jelly won't jell, that I think it would be a good idea to explain as simply as possible just what makes a good 'set' in jam, or a firm, sparkling fruit jelly. It is the presence of pectin, a natural gum-like substance in the pulp of fruit, that makes a jam or jelly set firmly. Acid in the fruit helps to extract pectin, so if a fruit is deficient in acid another fruit rich in acid (such as lemon, rhubarb, green apples, green gooseberries, redcurrants or blackcurrants) is added – or in the case of jelly making, citric or tartaric acid is used. Alternatively, commercially bottled pectin, known as Certo, can be used to aid setting when using fruits which are low in pectin.

Under-ripe fruit is richer in pectin and acid than fully ripe fruit; so you can see why it is better to use this for preserves.

When the fruit has been simmered to extract the pectin, the sugar is added. It is necessary that the fruit should be well broken down before sugar is added, because sugar has a hardening effect on fruit. But if you prefer to keep the fruit whole (as in the case of soft fruit), this toughening effect is an advantage. Simply sprinkle the sugar on the fruit overnight to extract the juice and pectin. Hard fruits must be simmered to break them down.

In jam making, it is only necessary to simmer the fruit long enough to break it up, since the pulp is to be kept in the preserve and, along with the pectin, acid and sugar, will help to give a firm set. Sugar is added after the first 20 minutes or so; the boiling of fruit pulp and sugar makes it almost certain that sufficient pectin will be extracted to set the jam. In jelly making only the juice is retained, so every scrap of pectin must be simmered out of the fruit before sugar is added.

As little water as possible should be added to the fruit; just enough to get it simmering. Until you know that there is sufficient pectin present to make a good set, it is not a bit of good adding your sugar, so test for pectin (see below) after the fruit has been simmering about 40 minutes.

You'll need a jelly bag for straining the juice. You can buy one, or make your own from cheap flannel or muslin. Don't press the fruit through the bag, but allow it to drip overnight. Extract more juice by turning the pulp from the bag into a little water, simmering it and then straining and mixing it with the first extraction.

Tackle only a small quantity of jelly making at a time; 2 pints (generous litre, 5 cups) of juice is enough for one go.

Sugar

Special preserving sugar, if you can get it, makes the best jams and jellies. Rather like broken lump (loaf) sugar, it gives a greater clearness to the preserve. Loaf sugar is the next best. Granulated sugar can also be used but it needs greater care in stirring until it is entirely dissolved.

Some proportion of brown sugar (say 25 per cent) may be added to dark jams such as blackcurrant, blackberry and damson, if preferred. Brown sugar gives a very good flavour but will darken and cloud the jam.

Pectin test

Take a teaspoon of the juice and add it to 3 teaspoons of methylated spirit, shake gently and leave for a minute or so. If there is plenty of pectin present, the juice will clot firmly; but if it stays liquid, or the clot is poor, the juice should be simmered longer.

Testing for a set

Even if you have tested for the pectin content of the juice before adding the sugar, it will be necessary to test the jam or jelly for setting point after fruit and sugar have been boiled for the time given in the recipes, or after 10 to 15 minutes. There are two ways a set can be tested:

1 Put a small spoonful of the jam on a cold saucer; stand saucer in a draught to cool. When quite cold, push the jam with the forefinger; if it wrinkles and a skin has formed on it, it has reached a good set. Don't take too long over this test or you will find the jam has over-cooked by the time you return to it.

2 Dip the stirring spoon in the jam, lift it and hold horizontally. If the juice forms a heavy clot, or flake, as it drips from the spoon, the jam is done.

Thermometer test

If you intend to take up jam or jelly making regularly, it is worthwhile buying a sugar boiling thermometer (not to be confused with a room heating thermometer). A thermometer marked up to 225°F./112°C. is suitable for jams or jellies, but one marked up to 312 to 350°F. (160 to 180°C.) is more practicable as it can then be used for sweets and toffee making, which have a higher setting point.

Before plunging the thermometer into boiling jam, heat it by dipping it into hot water. A good set has probably been reached if the thermometer shows 220°F./110°C., but to be on the safe side it is as well to boil the preserve a little longer, until 222°F./111°C. is shown. At the same time, I find it reassuring to use the cold saucer or the clot test in conjunction with the thermometer.

Six important points about jam and jelly making

1 Use sound, firm-ripe or slightly under-ripe fruit, gathered in dry weather, or bought dry.

2 Use a pan large enough to allow frothing up when sugar is added; use only enough water to start extraction of juice and pectin; with soft berry fruits use none at all.

3 **Simmer** the fruit until it is soft and all juice and pectin have been extracted.

4 Add heated sugar, stirring all the time, and do not allow the preserve to boil until sugar is dissolved.

5 Boil **rapidly**, after sugar has dissolved, until setting point is reached, testing after preserve has boiled for 10 minutes.

6 Skim only once, when jam is done. Allow to stand in pan for a few minutes, then stir and pot in heated jars; tie down at once, or when quite cold; never lukewarm.

Testing for a set using a sugar thermometer

Testing for a set by flake (clot) method

Recipes

Raspberry Jam

Yield approx 5–6 lb./2½ kg.

Imperial/Metric	American
3 lb./1½ kg. raspberries	3 lb. raspberries
½ pint/3 dl. redcurrant juice	1¼ cups red currant juice
3 lb./1½ kg. sugar	3 lb. sugar

Pick over the berries; rub them gently in a cloth to remove any leaves, etc. Do not wash them. Put berries and redcurrant juice in preserving pan; bring slowly to the boil. Add heated sugar, bring back to the boil after sugar dissolves. Boil quickly for 5 minutes. Put into jars and seal at once.

By using redcurrant juice, raspberry jam is a better colour, and the berries do not break down so much. However, this jam can be made without redcurrant juice. Do not use any water, but crush a few of the berries to extract juice, then add remaining berries and stir over heat until juice runs freely. Add heated sugar and stir gently until dissolved; bring to boil, and boil quickly for 5 minutes.

Shown in colour on page 51

Raspberry and Apple Jam

Yield approx 8–9 lb./4 kg.

Imperial/Metric	American
2 lb./1 kg. cooking apples, peeled, cored and sliced	2 lb. cooking apples, pared, cored and sliced
juice of 2 lemons	juice of 2 lemons
¼ pint/1½ dl. water	⅔ cup water
2 lb./1 kg. raspberries	2 lb. raspberries
4 lb./2 kg. sugar	4 lb. sugar

Simmer the apples in the lemon juice and water until tender, about 15 minutes. Add the cleaned raspberries and sugar and boil quickly until setting point is reached (see page 8). Pour into hot sterilised jars and seal immediately.

Strawberry Jam

Yield approx 6–7 lb./3 kg.

Imperial/Metric	American
4 lb./2 kg. strawberries	4 lb. strawberries
1 pint/6 dl. juice from stewed gooseberries, redcurrants or rhubarb	2½ cups juice from stewed gooseberries, red currants or rhubarb
4 lb./2 kg. sugar	4 lb. sugar

Pick over the strawberries, clean but don't wash them. It is best to toss or rub them lightly in a teatowel. Bring them to the boil with the juice, stirring gently, and allow to simmer for 10 minutes. Add the heated sugar, stir until sugar is melted and bring to the boil quickly. Boil rapidly for 3–4 minutes, then test for a set (see page 8). Boil a little longer, if necessary. Pot into hot sterilised jars, and tie down at once.

Strawberry Jam
using bottled pectin

Yield approx 5 lb./2¼ kg.

Imperial/Metric	American
2¾ lb./1¼ kg. strawberries	2¾ lb. strawberries
3 tablespoons lemon juice	4 tablespoons lemon juice
3 lb./1 kg. 400 g. sugar	3 lb. sugar
small knob of butter	small knob of butter
½ bottle pectin (Certo)	½ cup commercial pectin

Hull the fruit and crush thoroughly. Add the lemon juice and the sugar. Heat slowly until dissolved, stirring occasionally. Add small knob of butter or margarine to reduce foaming. Bring quickly to the boil and boil rapidly for 2 minutes, stirring occasionally. Remove from heat and stir in pectin – skim if necessary. Allow to cool slightly to prevent the fruit floating. Stir and then pot and cover in the usual way.

Plum and Apple Jam

Yield approx 10–11 lb./4½–5 kg.

Imperial/Metric	American
3 lb./1½ kg. apples, peeled, cored and sliced (place cores in muslin bag)	3 lb. apples, pared, cored and sliced (place cores in cheesecloth bag)
3 lb./1½ kg. plums, washed	3 lb. plums, washed
1 pint/6 dl. water	2½ cups water
6 lb./3 kg. sugar	6 lb. sugar
juice of 2 lemons	juice of 2 lemons
1 teaspoon cinnamon	1 teaspoon cinnamon

Place apple slices, cores and plums in a preserving pan. Add water and cook gently until reduced to a pulp, stirring occasionally. Add warmed sugar, lemon juice and cinnamon and continue cooking until jam sets when tested (see page 8). Remove cores. Pour into heated jars at once, cover closely and store in a cool place.

Plum and Elderberry Jam

Yield approx 6 lb./2¾ kg.

Imperial/Metric	American
2 lb./1 kg. elderberries	2 lb. elderberries
½ pint/3 dl. water	1¼ cups water
2½ lb./1¼ kg. plums	2½ lb. plums
4 lb./2 kg. preserving or lump sugar	4 lb. preserving or cube sugar

Stalk the elderberries and put into a pan with ¼ pint (1½ dl., ⅔ cup) of the water, bring to the boil and simmer for 3–4 minutes. Turn into a jelly bag to drip all night. Stone plums and cook until tender with rest of water, then add elder juice. Stir well and add sugar, previously warmed. Cook gently until dissolved, now boil rapidly and just before setting point is reached put in the kernels from the plum stones. Pot in warmed jars.

Plum or Greengage Jam

Yield approx 5–6 lb./2½ kg.

Imperial/Metric	American
3 lb./1½ kg. plums or greengages	3 lb. plums or greengages
½–¾ pint/3–4½ dl. water	1¼–2 cups water
3 lb./1½ kg. sugar	3 lb. sugar

Wash the fruit and stew slowly with the water until skins are softened. Ripe, juicy fruit requires less water than under-ripe fruit. Greengages need less cooking than plums; be careful not to boil them to a mash. Add sugar, stir until dissolved, bring to the boil and remove as many stones as possible as they rise to the surface. Boil rapidly until setting point is reached (see page 8).

The fruit may be stoned before cooking and the kernels cooked with the fruit.

Shown in colour on page 63

Cherry and Gooseberry Jam

Yield approx 6–7 lb./3 kg.

Imperial/Metric	American
2 lb./1 kg. sour red cherries or Morello cherries	2 lb. sour red cherries or Morello cherries
2 lb./1 kg. red gooseberries	2 lb. red gooseberries
juice of 3 lemons	juice of 3 lemons
4 lb./2 kg. sugar	4 lb. sugar

Wash fruit, top-and-tail gooseberries and stalk cherries. If you have time it is better to stone the cherries, but do it over a bowl to catch all the juice. Put into the preserving pan with strained lemon juice. Simmer for 30 minutes, removing any stones that come to the top. Add the heated sugar and stir over a low heat until it dissolves, then boil for 15–20 minutes or until a little jells, when tested (see page 8). Pour into heated jars and tie down at once.

Gooseberry Cheese

Yield approx 1–1½ lb./½–¾ kg.

Imperial/Metric	American
1 lb./½ kg. green gooseberries	1 lb. green gooseberries
2 tablespoons water	3 tablespoons water
4 oz./125 g. butter	½ cup butter
8 oz./225 g. sugar	1 cup sugar, firmly packed
pinch ground ginger	pinch ground ginger
2 eggs	2 eggs

Simmer gooseberries with water until soft, then rub through a sieve. Return pulp to pan, add butter, sugar, ginger and beaten eggs. Stir gently until it thickens, but do not allow to boil. Pour into small pots and cover.

This is a delicious filling for small tarts and flans, or it can be used as a filling for cakes; or a spoonful served as a sauce with plain blancmange. It is highly concentrated so you do not need a lot at a time to give flavour. Half quantities can be made.

Damson Cheese

Yield approx 1 lb./½ kg. to each 1 lb./½ kg. fruit pulp

Imperial/Metric	American
damsons	damsons
1 lb./½ kg. sugar to 1 lb./½ kg. of fruit pulp	1 lb. sugar to 1 lb. of fruit pulp

Stalk and wash as many damsons as you have. Put them in a stone jar or casserole, cover and place in a slow oven until juice runs, and stones are easily removed. Stir well; rub fruit through a sieve. Remove kernels from stones and add them to the pulp. Measure pulp and heat required amount of sugar. Mix sugar with pulp and put in a pan. Boil until it jells when tested, then pour into small jars. Put paper dipped in brandy (if possible) on top of each and tie down at once. Keep for 6 months before using it.

The cheese will shrink a little from sides of jars and have a crust of sugar. Instead of putting brandied paper on top, a bay leaf can be put on top of the cheese before tying down.

Blackcurrant and Apple Jam

Yield approx 7–8 lb./3½ kg.

Imperial/Metric	American
4 lb./2 kg. blackcurrants	4 lb. black currants
½ pint/3 dl. water	1¼ cups water
1½ lb./¾ kg. cooking apples	1½ lb. cooking apples
6 lb./3 kg. granulated or preserving sugar	6 lb. sugar

Put washed and stalked blackcurrants in preserving pan with half the water, and stew until tender. Peel, core and slice apples, put in a separate pan with rest of water, and cook until soft. Combine the pulps. (If seedless jam is required, sieve the blackcurrant pulp first.) Add sugar and stir over a low heat until dissolved. Bring to the boil and cook rapidly until setting point is reached – about 15 minutes (see page 8). Draw pan off heat, skim and put quickly into heated jars. Seal immediately.

Apple and Apricot Jam

Yield approx 5–6 lb./2½ kg.

Imperial/Metric	American
2 lb./1 kg. fresh apricots, halved and stoned	2 lb. fresh apricots, halved and pitted
2 lb./1 kg. apples, peeled, cored and chopped	2 lb. apples, pared, cored and chopped
1 pint/6 dl. water	2½ cups water
4 lb./2 kg. sugar	4 lb. sugar

Place all the ingredients in a saucepan and heat gently until sugar has dissolved. Bring to boil and cook for 30–40 minutes or until setting point is reached (see page 8. Stir frequently during cooking. Skim and pour into hot sterilised jars and cover.

Shown in colour on page 51

Apple and Fig Jam

Yield approx 7–8 lb./3½ kg.

Imperial/Metric	American
4 lb./2 kg. cooking apples	*4 lb. cooking apples*
2 lb./1 kg. figs, fresh or canned	*2 lb. figs, fresh or canned*
6 lb./3 kg. sugar	*6 lb. sugar*
1½ pints/9 dl. water	*3¾ cups water*

Peel, core and chop apples, chop figs. Place all ingredients in a saucepan and simmer for about 1 hour or until jam reaches setting point (see page 8). Pour into hot sterilised jars and cover.

Shown in colour on page 51

Blackberry and Apple Jam

Yield approx 4–5 lb./2 kg.

Imperial/Metric	American
2 lb./1 kg. cooking apples, peeled, cored and sliced	*2 lb. cooking apples, pared, cored and sliced*
¼ pint/1½ dl. water	*⅔ cup water*
juice of 2 lemons	*juice of 2 lemons*
2 lb./1 kg. blackberries	*2 lb. blackberries*
4 lb./2 kg. sugar	*4 lb. sugar*

Simmer the apples in water and lemon juice until tender, about 15 minutes. Add the blackberries and sugar and boil quickly until setting point is reached (see page 8). Pour into hot sterilised jars immediately and seal.

Green Tomato and Apple Jam

Yield approx 5½–6 lb./2½ kg.

Imperial/Metric	American
3 lb./1½ kg. green tomatoes	*3 lb. green tomatoes*
1–1½ pints/6–9 dl. water	*2½–3¾ cups water*
2 lb./1 kg. good cooking apples, peeled, cored and thinly sliced	*2 lb. good cooking apples, pared, cored and thinly sliced*
1½ teaspoons ground ginger	*1½ teaspoons ground ginger*
½ teaspoon ground cloves or a few whole cloves	*½ teaspoon ground cloves or a few whole cloves*
3½ lb./1¾ kg. sugar	*3½ lb. sugar*

Slice tomatoes thinly and place in pan with water. Cook for a short time before adding apples, ginger and cloves. When all are fairly soft, add warmed sugar, and boil quickly until the mixture will jell (see page 8). Pour into warmed jars and seal in the usual way.

Apple and Marrow Marmalade

Yield approx 7–8 lb./3½ kg.

Imperial/Metric	American
2 lb./1 kg. apples, after peeling and coring	*2 lb. apples, after paring and coring*
2 lb./1 kg. prepared marrow	*2 lb. prepared summer squash*
2 oz./50 g. crystallised ginger	*2 oz. candied ginger*
4 lb./2 kg. sugar	*4 lb. sugar*
grated rind and juice of 1 lemon	*grated rind and juice of 1 lemon*

Chop the prepared apples and marrow finely; chop the ginger. Mix the fruits and put them in a bowl in three layers with the sugar sprinkled between. Put lemon rind and juice on top. Leave overnight. Next day, give a good stir before putting into the preserving pan, and slowly bring to the boil. Boil for 30 minutes then test for setting (see page 8). Boil a little longer if necessary.

Pour into heated jars and tie down at once. Sour juicy apples should be used for this jam.

Marrow Preserve

Yield approx 4½–5 lb./2¼ kg.

Imperial/Metric	American
1½ lb./¾ kg. Bramley apples	*1½ lb. good cooking apples*
¼ pint/1½ dl. water	*⅔ cup water*
8 oz./225 g. golden syrup	*⅔ cup corn syrup*
1½ lb./¾ kg. sugar	*1½ lb. sugar*
2 teaspoons powdered ginger	*2 teaspoons powdered ginger*
1 orange	*1 orange*
1½ lb./¾ kg. marrow, peeled and diced	*1½ lb. summer squash, peeled and diced*

Peel the apples, quarter and cut away cores. Put into a preserving pan or large saucepan. Add the water, syrup, sugar and ginger. Grate the orange peel on to the other ingredients, using a fine side of a grater. Add the juice of the oranges. Bring slowly to the boil. Cut the marrow into small dice about ¼ inch/½ cm. square. Bring the preserve to the boil, and allow it to boil rapidly, stirring all the time, until it changes from a watery to a syrupy appearance. Add the marrow cubes and boil for another 6–10 minutes, testing frequently (see page 8).

The cubes should still be whole when the preserve is ready to be poured into hot jars and sealed.

Pear and Marrow Ginger

Yield approx 9–10 lb./4½ kg.

Imperial/Metric	American
1 marrow, about 3 lb./1½ kg. when peeled, seeded and diced	*1 summer squash, about 3 lb. when pared, seeded and diced*
¼ pint/1½ dl. water	*⅔ cup water*
1 piece root ginger	*1 piece root ginger*
3 lb./1½ kg. pears, peeled, cored and chopped	*3 lb. pears, pared, cored and chopped*
3 lb./1½ kg. sugar	*3 lb. sugar*
8 oz./225 g. preserved stem ginger, chopped	*2 cups Canton (preserved stem) ginger, chopped*

Simmer the marrow in the water, along with the root ginger, until tender. Remove the root ginger. Add the pears and sugar to the marrow, bring to the boil, add the stem ginger and continue boiling until setting point is reached (see page 8). Pour into sterilised jars and seal immediately.

Pear, Pineapple and Lemon Jam

Yield approx 6 lb./2¾ kg.

Imperial/Metric	American
3 lb./1½ kg. pears, peeled, cored and chopped	*3 lb. pears, pared, cored and chopped*
1 small pineapple, peeled and chopped	*1 small pineapple, pared and chopped*
juice and grated rind of 5 lemons	*juice and grated rind of 5 lemons*
4 lb./2 kg. preserving or granulated sugar	*4 lb. sugar*
miniature bottle of kirsch	*miniature bottle of kirsch*

Place all ingredients, except sugar and kirsch, into a large preserving pan, and simmer for 10 minutes. Add sugar and boil quickly until setting point is reached, then stir in kirsch. Reheat but do not boil. Pour into jars and seal.

Pear and Apricot Jam

Yield approx 7–8 lb./3½ kg.

Imperial/Metric	American
1 lb./½ kg. dried apricots	*1 lb. dried apricots*
3 lb./1½ kg. pears, peeled, cored and chopped	*3 lb. pears, pared, cored and chopped*
juice of 2 lemons	*juice of 2 lemons*
3½ lb./1¾ kg. preserving or granulated sugar	*3½ lb. sugar*

Soak apricots overnight. Drain, reserving water. Place apricots in a large preserving pan with the pears and lemon juice. Add a little of the reserved water. Simmer for 10 minutes. Add the sugar and boil quickly until setting point is reached (see page 8). Pour into hot sterilised jars. Seal at once, or when cold.

Shown in colour on page 51

Pear and Apricot De Luxe Preserve

Yield approx 5–6 lb./2½ kg.

Imperial/Metric	American
8 oz./225 g. dried apricots	*½ lb. dried apricots*
1½ pints/9 dl. water	*3¾ cups water*
1 lb./½ kg. sugar	*1 lb. sugar*
juice of 2 lemons	*juice of 2 lemons*
yellow food colouring	*yellow food coloring*
2 lb./1 kg. pears, peeled, cored and quartered	*2 lb. pears, pared, cored and quartered*
3 tablespoons Grand Marnier	*4 tablespoons Grand Marnier*

Soak the apricots for 6 hours in the water. Drain. Dissolve sugar in lemon juice and water. Bring to the boil and simmer until syrupy. Tint syrup with a little yellow colouring. Add the pear quarters and the drained apricots, and simmer until fruit is plumped and just tender. Stir in the Grand Marnier, bring quickly to the boil, then pour into hot sterilised jars. Seal immediately.

Apricot Butter

Yield approx 1 lb./½ kg.

Imperial/Metric	American
2 oz./50 g. dried apricots	*⅓ cup dried apricots*
pinch bicarbonate of soda	*pinch baking soda*
water to cover	*water to cover*
8 oz./225 g. castor sugar	*1 cup granulated sugar, firmly packed*
2 oz./50 g. butter	*¼ cup butter*
2 eggs, well beaten	*2 eggs, well beaten*
grated rind and juice of ½ lemon	*grated rind and juice of ½ lemon*

Wash and cut apricots, place in a bowl. Add bicarbonate of soda and then enough boiling water to cover apricots. Stand for 1 hour or longer, drain off water and reserve. Rinse apricots in cold water, then cook in as little apricot-soaked water as possible, until tender. Pass through a sieve, add the sugar, butter and eggs, lemon rind and juice. Stand in a basin in pan of boiling water and cook over low heat, stirring all the time until thick. Pour into a clean hot jar, and tie down at once.

Double the quantities to make more. The consistency should be the same as lemon curd.

Sage and Apple Butter

Yield approx 6 lb./2¾ kg.

Imperial/Metric	American
4 lb./2 kg. cooking apples, peeled, cored and sliced	4 lb. cooking apples, pared, cored and sliced
8 oz./225 g. sugar	1 cup sugar
2 teaspoons salt	2 teaspoons salt
2 teaspoons pepper	2 teaspoons pepper
3 teaspoons dried sage	3 teaspoons dried sage
1 onion, finely chopped	1 onion, finely chopped
¼ pint/1½ dl. water	⅔ cup water
2 oz./50 g. butter	¼ cup butter
1 teaspoon Worcestershire sauce	1 teaspoon Worcestershire sauce
3 tablespoons vinegar	4 tablespoons vinegar

Simmer all ingredients together over a gentle heat until apples are pulpy. Beat until creamy. Pour into sterilised jars and seal.

Apple and Cinnamon Butter

Yield approx 3½–4 lb./1¾ kg.

Imperial/Metric	American
4 lb./2 kg. cooking apples, peeled, cored and sliced	4 lb. cooking apples, pared, cored and sliced
2 oz./50 g. butter	¼ cup butter
7 oz./200 g. sugar	scant 1 cup sugar
3 teaspoons powdered cinnamon	3 teaspoons powdered cinnamon
4 whole cloves	4 whole cloves
½ pint/3 dl. water	1¼ cups water

Simmer all the ingredients in a covered saucepan until apples are quite tender. Remove cloves. Beat until creamy, heat until boiling, bottle and seal immediately.

Shown in colour on page 51

Rhubarb and Loganberry Jam

Yield approx 7–8 lb./3½ kg.

Imperial/Metric	American
3 lb./1½ kg. red rhubarb	3 lb. red rhubarb
about ½ pint/3 dl. water	about 1¼ cups water
2 lb./1 kg. loganberries	2 lb. loganberries
5 lb./2½ kg. sugar	5 lb. sugar

Use only the red parts of rhubarb. Wipe and cut up roughly and stew in the water until reduced to a pulp. Stir well to prevent sticking. Pick over the loganberries and wash them. Put them in a pan and crush slightly to make juice run, then simmer for a few minutes, pressing well with a wooden spoon. Mix the two fruits, add the heated sugar, and stir over low heat until sugar dissolves, then boil rapidly until jam sets (see page 8). Pour into hot jars and seal at once.

Spring Rhubarb and Carrot Conserve

Yield approx 2½–3 lb./1¼–1½ kg.

Imperial/Metric	American
1 lb./½ kg. spring carrots	1 lb. young carrots
1 lb./½ kg. early rhubarb	1 lb. young rhubarb
1 lemon	1 lemon
4 oz./125 g. candied citron peel	¾ cup candied citron peel
water to cover	water to cover
2 lb./1 kg. granulated sugar	2 lb. sugar
½ oz./15 g. crystallised ginger, chopped	½ oz. crystallized ginger, chopped

Wash carrots, rhubarb and lemon and dry well. Cut carrots into small pieces, and rhubarb into 1-inch/2½-cm. pieces (do not peel). Shred the citron peel. Grate yellow part of lemon, then remove the white skin. Cut up pulp finely, removing the pips and pith. Cook carrots, rhubarb and lemon in water to just cover, until tender. Then add sugar, citron peel, lemon peel and chopped ginger. Stir over low heat until sugar melts, then boil up quickly until jam sets when tested (see page 8). Stir often. Pour into heated jars and cover at once.

Pumpkin and Apricot Jam

Yield approx 6–7 lb./3 kg.

Imperial/Metric	American
1 lb./½ kg. dried apricots	1 lb. dried apricots
2 lb./1 kg. pumpkin	2 lb. pumpkin
1½ lb./¾ kg. sugar (for sprinkling pumpkin)	1½ lb. sugar (for sprinkling pumpkin)
2½ lb./1¼ kg. extra sugar	2½ lb. extra sugar
½ teaspoon ground ginger or ½ oz./15 g. crystallised ginger, chopped	½ teaspoon ground ginger or ½ oz. crystallized ginger, chopped

Soak the apricots in water to barely cover. Peel and chop pumpkin into small dice, cover with 1½ lb./¾ kg. sugar. Leave both the apricots and pumpkin to stand like this for 24 hours. Next day, put apricots with their liquor, the pumpkin, the remaining sugar and the ginger into preserving pan and mix well. Bring slowly to the boil, stirring until sugar melts. Cook slowly until pumpkin is tender, then boil rapidly until mixture jells when tested (see page 8). Pot into hot jars, and tie down when cold.

Bramble and Apple Jelly

Yield approx 8–9 lb./4 kg.

Imperial/Metric	American
6 lb./2¾ kg. blackberries	6 lb. blackberries
3 lb./1½ kg. tart cooking apples	3 lb. tart cooking apples
2½–3 pints/1¼–1½ litres water	6¼–7½ cups water
sugar	sugar

Blackberries should be just ripe. Wash, drain well then put in preserving pan. Add apples, washed and roughly chopped, but not peeled or cored. Pour in water to just cover the fruit when it is shaken down in pan. Bring fruit to boil then simmer gently for 25–30 minutes. When fruit is tender and a quarter to one-third of the liquid has evaporated, mash the fruit thoroughly in the pan. Turn the mash into a jelly or muslin bag, and leave over a basin to drip overnight.

Next day, measure juice and put into clean preserving pan. For each 1 pint (6 dl., 2½ cups) of juice allow 1 lb./½ kg. sugar. Bring juice to the boil and stir in heated sugar gradually. When all sugar has dissolved bring to a full rolling boil and boil rapidly until setting point is reached, in about 10 minutes (see page 8). Skim quickly then pot at once in clean, hot jars. Cover when cold. Jelly should not be tilted until it is quite set.

If smaller quantities are wanted, reduce all ingredients by half except water when 1½ pints (9 dl., 3¾ cups) should be used.

Shown in colour on page 63

Below Preparing the fruit *Top right* Straining pulp in a jelly bag *Centre right* When ready, jelly crinkles against back of finger when pushed *Bottom right* Serve with cream as dessert, or with scones for tea

Apple Jelly

Yield approx 6 lb./2¾ kg.

Imperial/Metric	American
6 lb./3 kg. cooking apples	6 lb. cooking apples
3 cloves	3 cloves
4 lb./2 kg. sugar (approx)	4 lb. sugar (approx)

Cut the apples into quarters without peeling or coring and cover with cold water in a saucepan. Add cloves. Bring to the boil and cook gently, but thoroughly. Put apples in a strainer with a muslin lining and drain overnight.

Measure the liquid and add 1 lb./½ kg. sugar to every 1 pint (6 dl., 2½ cups) liquid. Heat slowly to dissolve sugar, then bring to the boil and allow to boil rapidly until the jelly will set when tested (see page 8). The green apple liquid will change to a soft amber during the cooking time.

Spiced Rowan Jelly

Yield approx 4lb./2 kg.

Imperial/Metric	American
2 lb./1 kg. green apples	2 lb. green apples
2 lb./1 kg. rowanberries, stalked	2 lb. rowanberries (mountain ash), stalked
juice and rind of 1 lemon	juice and rind of 1 lemon
1 teaspoon cloves	1 teaspoon cloves
sugar	sugar

Wash and cut up apples, removing bruises, but not peeling or coring. Put them with all other ingredients, except sugar, into preserving pan, cover with water and boil to a pulp. Put pulp in a jelly bag and strain overnight. Allow 1 lb./½ kg. sugar to each 1 pint (6 dl., 2½ cups) of juice, and boil until it jells when tested (see page 8). The jelly is slightly bitter and is excellent with hare, rabbit, mutton or grouse.

Grape Jelly

Yield approx 5–5½ lb./2½ kg.

Imperial/Metric	American
3 lb./1½ kg. fully-ripe grapes	3 lb. fully-ripe grapes
¼ pint/1½ dl. water	⅔ cup water
sugar	sugar
1 lemon	1 lemon
½ bottle pectin (Certo)	½ cup commercial pectin

With scissors, snip the grapes from the main stalks of the bunches; small ends of stalks may be left on. Crush grapes well in large saucepan. Add water, bring to boil and simmer 10 minutes. Strain through jelly bag or muslin square and leave to drip into basin overnight. Put sugar (for each 1 pint (6 dl., 2½ cups) of juice allow 1 lb./½ kg. sugar) and juice into large saucepan with juice of the lemon. Heat slowly until sugar is dissolved, stirring often. Bring quickly to the boil, and at once add the pectin, stirring all the time. Bring to a full rolling boil, and allow to boil for about ½ minute, skim and pour into small jars. Cover at once.

Clear Mint Jelly

Yield approx 1½ pints/scant litre/3¾ cups

Imperial/Metric	American
4 lb./2 kg..rhubarb	4 lb. rhubarb
2 pints/generous litre water	5 cups water
2 lemons	2 lemons
4 tablespoons chopped mint	5 tablespoons chopped mint
1 lb./½ kg. sugar to each 1 pint/6 dl. of juice	1 lb. sugar to each 2½ cups of juice
few drops green food colouring	few drops green food coloring
few drops oil of peppermint	few drops oil of peppermint

Wipe and chop rhubarb. Simmer with water and lemon juice for 30–40 minutes; add the mint, stir well and boil for a minute or so longer. Strain through a jelly or muslin bag overnight. Measure for sugar. Heat the juice and warmed sugar. Stir until dissolved, boil rapidly until setting point is reached (see page 8). Remove from heat, cool a little, and add a few drops of green colouring and oil of peppermint. Pot into small jars. *Oil* of peppermint must be used (not essence). It can be bought from chemists.

Apple Ginger

Yield approx 4½–5 lb./2¼ kg.

Imperial/Metric	American
4 lb./2 kg. firm juicy apples	4 lb. firm juicy apples
4 lb./2 kg. sugar	4 lb. sugar
2 pints/generous litre water	5 cups water
2 oz./50 g. essence of ginger	2 oz. essence of ginger

Peel the fruit, remove core, and cut fruit into chunky pieces. Boil sugar and water together until it forms a syrup (this will take 20–25 minutes), then put in the apples a few at a time so that the syrup does not go off the boil. When all the apples are in and the mixture well boiling add the essence of ginger, and boil gently, stirring as little as possible, until the preserve clears and becomes yellow. This will take 45 minutes to 1 hour. Skim well, and put into small jars, and tie down when cold.

Lemon Curd

Yield approx 1 lb./½ kg.

Imperial/Metric	American
4 oz./125 g. butter	½ cup butter
8 oz./225 g. granulated sugar	1 cup sugar
3 eggs	3 eggs
grated rind and juice of 2 lemons	grated rind and juice of 2 lemons

Melt butter in top part of double saucepan, placed over low heat. Add sugar slowly and stir until well blended. Beat eggs and pour them gradually into the butter and sugar. Stir until mixture is light and creamy; do not allow it to get very hot. Grate the yellow peel from the lemons and add it to the mixture. Squeeze the juice from the lemons and strain, add slowly, stirring all the time. Place the pan over the lower part of double saucepan with boiling water in it, over low heat, and stir until the curd forms a film on back of spoon. Pour into screw-top jar.

Shown in colour on page 59

Slowly add sugar to melted butter in top of double saucepan, then add beaten eggs gradually

Grate lemon peel, then squeeze juice and add

Curd forms film on spoon when ready

Apple and Raspberry Curd

Yield approx 6 lb./2¾ kg.

Imperial/Metric	American
3½ lb./1½ kg. cooking apples, peeled, cored and chopped	3½ lb. cooking apples, pared, cored and chopped
juice and grated rind of 3 lemons	juice and grated rind of 3 lemons
1½ lb./¾ kg. raspberries, fresh or frozen	1½ lb. raspberries, fresh or frozen
10 oz./275 g. butter	1¼ cups butter
5 eggs, beaten	5 eggs, beaten
1¾ lb./800 g. sugar	1¾ lb. sugar
scant ½ pint/2½ dl. water	1 cup water

Simmer apples with lemon juice and rind until tender. Beat until smooth. Heat fresh raspberries gently in a saucepan to extract the juices and simmer until soft. If frozen raspberries are used this is not necessary. Sieve to remove the seeds. Combine raspberry and apple mixtures, and place in large double saucepan. Add butter, beaten eggs, sugar and water, and cook over boiling water until thick. Pour into sterilised jars and seal.

H P—B

Tangerine Jelly and Tangerine Conserve
made from the same fruit

Yield approx 6 lb./2¾ kg. and 3½ lb./1¾ kg. conserve

Imperial/Metric	American
3 lb./1½ kg. tangerines	3 lb. tangerines
1 large lemon	1 large lemon
½ oz./15 g. citric acid	½ oz. citric acid
4½ pints/2¾ litres water	5¾ pints water
3½ lb./1¾ kg. sugar	3½ lb. sugar

Wash and peel fruit and shred peels finely. Cut fruit in slices and tie pips loosely, but securely, in muslin. Soak peel, fruit and juice, citric acid and bag of pips in the water overnight, and then simmer for about 1½ hours or until lemon peel is tender. Strain the fruit through a jelly bag or muslin overnight. (The peels and pulp remaining are used to make Tangerine Conserve, see below.)

Boil up fruit juice in the preserving pan, add the sugar, stir over low heat until melted. Then boil rapidly for about 20 minutes, until setting point is reached (see page 8). Pot and tie down when cold.

To strain fruit through muslin
Select a kitchen chair that has no cross-bar underneath, and place upside-down with the seat resting on the kitchen table. Tie a strong clean cloth with string to the four feet of the chair legs, and put a bowl underneath to catch the juice. Pour fruit and juice into the improvised jelly bag and leave overnight to drain.

Tangerine Conserve

Yield approx as above

Imperial/Metric	American
the peels and pulp left over from the tangerine jelly (above)	the peels and pulp left over from the tangerine jelly (above)
juice of 1 lemon	juice of 1 lemon
½ pint/3 dl. water	1¼ cups water
2¼ lb./1 kg sugar	2¼ lb. sugar

Put the fruit pulp, lemon juice and water in pan. Remove bag of pips, squeezing all juice possible from it back into the pan. Bring to boiling point, add sugar and stir over low heat until melted. Then bring to boil, and allow to boil briskly for about 15 minutes to setting point (see page 8). Pot and tie down when cold.

 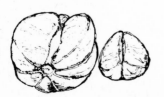

Apple Slices in Wine and Lemon Syrup

Yield approx 3 2-pint (1-litre, 2½-pint) jars

Imperial/Metric	American
8 lemons	8 lemons
1 pint/6 dl. boiling water	2½ cups boiling water
1 pint/6 dl. white wine	2½ cups white wine
4½ lb./2 kg. preserving or granulated sugar	4½ lb. sugar
4 lb./1¾ kg. apples, peeled, cored and sliced	4 lb. apples, pared, cored and sliced
2 tablespoons brandy	3 tablespoons brandy
yellow colouring (optional)	yellow coloring (optional)

Pare the rind from the lemons and place in a large bowl. Cover with the boiling water and white wine and allow to infuse for 30 minutes. Place in a preserving pan, with the juice from the lemons, and the sugar. Boil for 8 minutes. Strain to remove the lemon rind. Return the lemon syrup to the pan with the apples, and cook until apples are just tender and syrup is thick. Stir in brandy and reheat. Pour into hot sterilised preserving jars, and seal. The syrup may be tinted with a little yellow food colouring if liked.

Marrons Glacés
Glazed Sweet Chestnuts

Prepare fresh, large nuts by slitting each down one side with a pointed knife. Put in a pan with water to cover and boil until tender, about 20 minutes. Shell the nuts, removing inner and outer skins; they must be kept in the hot water while this is being done, as it is impossible to shell the nuts when they are cold. As the nuts are shelled, drop them into warm water with a little lemon juice added.

Make a plain syrup using two parts sugar to one of water, boiling it until it coats the back of a spoon. Drain the nuts and dry them well in a tea-cloth. Put them in the syrup and boil until quite tender, but unbroken. Remove and drain on a wire cake rack. Boil syrup to the 'crack' stage – a little dropped in cold water should set hard at once – remove pan from the heat and dip the chestnuts one by one, on a skewer or knitting needle, into the syrup. Hold each nut in the syrup until thoroughly coated, place on the wire rack and dry them off on a low shelf in a very cool oven (150°F., 65°C., less than Gas Mark ¼). Put each chestnut in a wax paper case and arrange in single layers in a fancy box, or on shallow glass dishes.

Making strawberry jam, see recipe, page 9

Mincemeat

Yield approx 2 1-lb./½-kg. jars

Imperial/Metric	American
8 oz./225 g. currants	1½ cups currants
8 oz./225 g. sultanas	1½ cups seedless white raisins
4 oz./125 g. muscatel raisins, chopped	¾ cup chopped muscatel raisins
2 oz./50 g. blanched almonds, chopped	½ cup chopped blanched almonds
4 oz./125 g. chopped peel	1 cup chopped candied peel
6 oz./175 g. brown sugar	⅔ cup brown sugar
8 oz./225 g. shredded suet	½ lb. finely chopped beef suet
2 large juicy apples, grated	2 large juicy apples, grated
rind and juice of 1 lemon and 1 orange	rind and juice of 1 lemon and 1 orange
1 teaspoon mixed cake spice	1 teaspoon mixed spices
¼ teaspoon grated nutmeg	¼ teaspoon grated nutmeg
½ teaspoon salt	½ teaspoon salt
1 tablespoon sherry or rum	1 tablespoon sherry or rum

Wash and thoroughly dry the fruits, and mix them well together with the nuts, peel, sugar, suet, apple, grated lemon and orange rinds, spices and salt. Add the orange and lemon juice, stir well and leave until next day. Then add the sherry or rum, mix thoroughly, and put into jars. Seal with airtight covers.

Mix mincemeat a little on the dry side, then add a little sherry, rum or orange juice when making mince pies.

Shown in colour on page 31

Spiced Pear Mincemeat

Yield approx 7 lb./3¼ kg.

Imperial/Metric	American
1½ lb./¾ kg. pears, peeled, cored and chopped	1½ lb. pears, pared, cored and chopped
1 lb./450 g. currants	1 lb. currants
1 lb./450 g. raisins	1 lb. raisins
8 oz./225 g. glacé apricots, chopped	1½ cups chopped candied apricots
12 oz./350 g. mixed peel	2 cups candied peel
12 oz./350 g. shredded suet	¾ lb. finely chopped beef suet
1 lb./½ kg. brown sugar	2 cups brown sugar
2 heaped tablespoons mixed spice	3 heaped tablespoons mixed spices
2 heaped tablespoons cinnamon	3 heaped tablespoons cinnamon
1 heaped tablespoon ground ginger	1 heaped tablespoon ground ginger
1 heaped tablespoon ground cloves	1 heaped tablespoon ground cloves
2 or 3 tablespoons brandy (optional)	3 or 4 tablespoons brandy (optional)
sherry to mix	sherry to mix

Combine all ingredients, and mix thoroughly. Turn into sterilised jars and seal.

Rose Petal Conserve

Yield approx 1 lb./½ kg.

Imperial/Metric	American
1 lb./½ kg. red rose petals (old fashioned cabbage roses are best)	1 lb. red rose petals (old fashioned cabbage roses are best)
1 lb./½ kg. granulated sugar	1 lb. granulated sugar
¼ pint/1½ dl. rose water	⅔ cup rose water
1 tablespoon orange-flower water	1 tablespoon orange-flower water

Separate the petals, removing yellow centres of flowers; spread petals out to dry in the sun. Put them in a strainer or piece of muslin and dip them in boiling water for a second or so; drain and dry them. Make a light syrup with the sugar, rose water and orange-flower water, put in the rose petals and simmer until the conserve is quite thick and soft, stirring occasionally; this will take 30–45 minutes. Pour into small pots with wide necks; cover with wax paper. In the old days it was poured into little fancy china dishes, ready for the tea table.

Note

Chemists usually stock rose water and orange-flower water.

Home-made Candied Peel

Imperial/Metric	American
peel of 4 sweet oranges	peel of 4 sweet oranges
½ oz./15 g. bicarbonate of soda	½ oz. baking soda
water	water
granulated sugar	granulated sugar

Wash the oranges. Remove the peel in quarters by cutting with a sharp-pointed knife through the peel right round the orange, starting at the stalk end, then cut in the opposite direction to quarter it. Remove as much loose pith as possible from inside the peel. Soak the peel in a solution of bicarbonate of soda and 2 pints (1¼ litres, 5 cups) water for 20–30 minutes, then strain away the water, cover the peel with fresh water and simmer until tender, about 30 minutes. Now make a sugar syrup with 8 oz./225 g. sugar and ½ pint (3 dl., 1¼ cups) of the water in which the peel was boiled, add the drained peel and simmer for about 30 minutes, until transparent and the syrup thickens. Remove the peel on to a wire cake rack to drain, overnight. Boil up the syrup again and drop the peel into it; take up on to the rack and leave to dry. Roll the peel in granulated sugar and store in covered jar in a cool place. The peel keeps for 3–4 months. Lemon peel can be treated in the same way.

Marmalade

The best time to make marmalade is at the end of January or early February, when Seville oranges are about, and all other citrus fruit – Jaffa and navel oranges, lemons, Jaffa grapefruit – are at their best and most plentiful.

There are several kinds of bitter oranges available at this time; some come from Malaga or Sicily and other Mediterranean islands or countries; but connoisseurs of marmalade believe that Seville oranges are the only ones to use, even though they may be a little more expensive than the others. Their skins are a deep, reddish orange, free from blemishes, giving a rich deep golden-brown colour to the marmalade; they are usually juicier, and experts say that they have the correct proportion of pips necessary for the supply of pectin, and that the inner skins are more tender.

To soak or not to soak? There are two schools of thought about this. The first says that the fruit should be sliced without removing the peel, but removing centre pith and pips; the fruit is soaked in the correct amount of water overnight, and the pith and pips (the chief source of pectin) soaked separately.

The second school says that soaking is unnecessary, the fruit being boiled whole until tender – a long process – then it is chopped up roughly, the pips and excess pith being removed at the same time. Fruit pulp and liquid are then brought to the boil, the sugar added, and simmered until sugar dissolves, then boiled quickly until setting point is reached.

There are also differences of opinion on how the fruit is prepared for the soaking method – some people say halve the fruit and squeeze out the juice, then chop the peel or put it through a mincer; while others prefer to quarter the oranges and cut them in thin slices downwards. So you can take your choice.

The really famous firms of commercial marmalade-makers in England, say that to get a good 'home-made' marmalade the fruit must be cut up and soaked for 24 hours or longer, and the boiling is done in relatively small domestic containers. Machines can't do what women do by hand – removing pith and pips, etc. In short, you can't make good marmalade in a hurry, or in vast quantities at a time. Naturally their product is rather more expensive than marmalade you make at home; if you and your family are toast and marmalade addicts you will see that it really does pay to make your own.

What are the advantages of soaking? It makes the fruit swell and softens it, so that the pectin is more quickly extracted, and the peel softened. If you do not soak the fruit, the marmalade will have to be boiled for a longer time *before* the sugar is added. After the sugar is added the fruit will not soften any more, and no amount of boiling will make the peel more tender or make the marmalade more likely to set. Overboiling will only make it syrupy and a bad colour and, what is more, it will not keep well.

After setting point has been reached, marmalade should always be allowed to stand in the pan until a slight skin forms on top, then it is well stirred to distribute the fruit evenly before being potted. Marmalade is best potted in small jars, as it loses flavour and colour when exposed to light and air; always store in a cool, dark cupboard.

The most modern, and really time-saving way of making marmalade is in a pressure cooker. For this method much less water is needed for cooking the oranges – about half the usual amount – and the fruit does not need soaking. Whatever make of pressure cooker you use, special instructions will be given for making preserves, and you should follow these; however, general instructions are given for making a variety of marmalades in a special section beginning on page 25.

Old English Breakfast Marmalade

Yield approx 5 lb./2¼ kg.

Imperial/Metric	American
6 Seville oranges	6 Seville oranges
2 large lemons	2 large lemons
4 pints/2¼ litres water	10 cups (5 pints) water
6 lb./2 kg. 700 g. sugar	6 lb. sugar

Wash the oranges and lemons well. Cut them into quarters, remove centre pith. Put pith and all pips into a small basin. Cut the fruit into thin slices, taking care to catch all juice. Put the fruit as you cut it into a large earthenware bowl. Pour 3½ pints (2 litres, 9 cups) of water over the fruit and the remaining water over the pips and pith. Leave to stand for 24 hours.

Pour fruit and water into preserving pan, and strain the water from the pips into the pan. Tie the pips and pith in a piece of muslin, and tie this to the handle of the pan so it is suspended in the liquid. Simmer until the liquid is reduced by half, and the peel is tender. This will take 1½–2 hours. Then detach the bag of pips and press it against the side of the pan to remove all juice. Add the heated sugar gradually to the fruit, stirring all the time until the sugar is dissolved. It is most important that the preserve does not boil until sugar is quite dissolved. Then bring quickly to the boil, and keep at a good rolling boil for 10 minutes. Test for a set (see page 8). Boil for a little longer, if required.

When ready, allow the marmalade to stand in the pan for a few minutes, then stir well, and pot in hot, dry jars. Cover with wax discs and transparent circles secured with rubber bands, either immediately, or leave until quite cold. Never cover when warm.

Old English Marmalade

Yield approx 5 lb./2¼ kg.

Imperial/Metric	American
6 bitter oranges	6 bitter oranges
1 large sweet orange	1 large sweet orange
2 lemons	2 lemons
6 pints/3½ litres water	15½ cups (7½ pints) water
6 lb./2 kg. 700 g. sugar	6 lb. sugar

Wash oranges and lemons well; pare off yellow rind taking as little pith as possible. Cut the yellow rind into chunky pieces; put these in preserving pan. Remove white pith from outside fruit, put into large basin. Cut fruit pulp into rough pieces, removing pith and pips and any coarse skin as you do so. Put pulp into preserving pan; pith and pips into basin with outer pith. Pour 5 pints (3 litres, 6½ pints) of water into preserving pan; pour the remaining water into basin with pith and pips.

Cover and leave for 24 hours. Then strain water from basin into preserving pan; tie pith and pips in piece of muslin, and tie this to handle of preserving pan so that it is suspended in water. Bring to the boil and boil gently for 1 hour longer – until skins are tender and the liquid is reduced by about half. Stir frequently while boiling, to prevent sticking; remove scum after the hour's boiling. Now add the sugar and simmer 20–30 minutes, stirring frequently. Remove pip and pith bag, squeezing it well; boil up marmalade quickly, cook until quantity is reduced to about half, remove last of scum.

Test the marmalade (see page 8). A little longer boiling may be necessary, but do not boil for long without testing at this stage, as overboiling will make the marmalade dark and treacly. When done, leave in the pan until marmalade begins to skin over; then stir well, and pour into heated jars. When quite cold, cover securely.

Preparing fruit for marmalade, see recipe above

Seville Orange Marmalade
using bottled pectin

Yield approx 9–10 lb./4½ kg.

Imperial/Metric	American
2½ lb./1¼ kg. bitter oranges	2½ lb. bitter oranges
2 lemons	2 lemons
2 pints/generous litre water	5 cups water
1 level teaspoon bicarbonate of soda	1 teaspoon baking soda
5 lb./2¼ kg. sugar	5 lb. sugar
small piece butter or margarine	small piece butter or margarine
1 bottle pectin	1 cup commercial pectin

Wash fruit and remove peel in quarters using sharp knife. Scrape off and discard about half of the white part. Shred peel very finely, and place in preserving pan with water and soda. Bring to the boil and simmer covered, but stirring occasionally, for 10–15 minutes, or until the peel can be crushed easily between thumb and forefinger. Cut up the peeled fruit, discarding the pips and tough skin. Add pulp and juice to cooked rind. Simmer covered for a further 20 minutes.

Put sugar and 3 pints (1½ litres, 7½ cups) prepared fruit into large preserving pan, making up the quantity with water if necessary. Heat slowly, stirring occasionally, until the sugar has dissolved. Add small piece of butter or margarine. Bring to a full rolling boil and boil for 5 minutes. Remove preserving pan from heat and stir in pectin. Then stir and skim and leave for just 7 minutes to cool slightly to prevent fruit floating. Pour into clean hot jars and cover.

Jelly Marmalade

Yield approx 4–5 lb./2 kg.

Imperial/Metric	American
6 Seville oranges	6 Seville oranges
1 large sweet orange	1 large sweet orange
1 lemon	1 lemon
5 pints/3 litres water	13 cups (6½ pints) water
sugar	sugar

Thinly peel the fruit with a knife, then cut into match-like strips. Tie these in a muslin bag allowing room to swell. Remove as much as possible of the white inner pith from fruit. Cut up the pulp roughly, making 3 or 4 slices out of each. Put the fruit into a preserving pan with the strips of peel in the bag, and add the water. Leave overnight. Next day, boil steadily for 2–2½ hours, stirring from time to time. Remove bag of peel, and empty peel into a basin. Strain the pulp twice through a fine sieve, return the peel to liquid, measure it and add 1¼ lb. (600 g., 2¼ cups) sugar to each 1 pint (6 dl., 2½ cups) of liquid.

Rinse out preserving pan, put in sugar and the liquid, stir over low heat until sugar melts, then bring to the boil and boil steadily until jelly sets when tested on cold plate (see page 8). This will take at least 25 minutes. Allow to stand in pan 30 minutes, stirring from time to time, then pour off into jars. Leave until quite cold before tying down.

Shown in colour on page 27

Lemon Marmalade

Yield approx 5 lb./2¼ kg.

Imperial/Metric	American
1½ lb./¾ kg. fresh lemons	1½ lb. fresh lemons
3 pints/1½ litres water	7½ cups water
3 lb./1 kg. 400 g. sugar	3 lb. sugar

Wash the fruit, take off the yellow rind and cut into fine shreds. Remove all white pith and cut into rough pieces. Slice the pulp, removing pips and any hard parts of the core, and tie pith, pips and other trimmings loosely but securely in a muslin bag. Soak all overnight in the water. Next day, boil for about 1 hour or until the shreds of peel are quite tender. Remove the bag, squeeze out all possible juice from it and add to the pan with the sugar.

Stir until the sugar has dissolved, and then boil briskly until setting point is reached (see page 8). Remove from the heat and leave until a slight skin forms on the top. Stir gently to distribute the peel, pot and cover at once.

Four Fruit Marmalade
using bottled pectin

Yield approx 8 lb./3¾ kg.

Imperial/Metric	American
3¼ lb./1½ kg. fruit made up from:	3¼ lb. fruit made up from:
1 grapefruit	1 grapefruit
2 sweet oranges	2 sweet oranges
3 large lemons	3 large lemons
2 apples	2 apples
1½ pints/9 dl. water	3¾ cups water
¼ level teaspoon bicarbonate of soda	¼ teaspoon baking soda
5 lb./2¼ kg. sugar	5 lb. sugar
1 bottle pectin	1 cup commercial pectin

Wash and peel the citrus fruit, discarding about half the white pith. Slice the peel finely and place in saucepan with water and bicarbonate of soda. Simmer, covered, for 10–15 minutes. Peel and core apples and cut into small cubes. Cut up the peeled citrus fruit, discarding the pips and tough skin. Catch all juice that is pressed out. Add fruit and juice to rind and continue simmering covered, for a further 20 minutes.

Measure the hot fruit into a large saucepan and, if necessary, make it up to 1½ pints (9 dl., 3¾ cups) by addition of water. Add the sugar and heat gently, stirring occasionally until the sugar has dissolved. Bring to a full rolling boil and boil rapidly for 3 minutes. Remove from heat and stir in pectin, boil again for 1 minute. Leave to cool to prevent fruit floating. Skim, stir well, pot and cover while hot.

Tomato Marmalade

Yield approx 6–7 lb./3 kg.

Imperial/Metric	American
4 lb./2 kg. fully-ripe tomatoes	4 lb. fully-ripe tomatoes
3 lemons	3 lemons
½ pint/3 dl. water	1¼ cups water
4 lb./2 kg. preserving or lump sugar	4 lb. preserving or cube sugar

Pour boiling water over tomatoes, remove skins and stalk ends. Cut into thick slices. Slice lemons, removing pips. Put sugar in preserving pan with the water, heat slowly until sugar has dissolved, then boil rapidly for 6 minutes. Add tomatoes and lemons and boil steadily until marmalade is thick enough to set, about 30–40 minutes. Remove lemon rind and scum as it rises. When done, allow to cool slightly, then stir well and pot in hot jars. Tie down at once.

General instructions for marmalade-making in a pressure cooker

Use the 10 lb./5 kg. pressure control – and *never have the pressure cooker more than half full*. Pressure cook *fruit only*. Proceed in open cooker after sugar has been added.

1 Wash and peel fruit. Remove pith and pips and tie loosely in muslin bag. Shred peel according to taste. Cut up fruit roughly.

2 Remove trivet, then put the water, fruit, peel and muslin bag into the pressure cooker.

3 Cover, bring to 10 lb./5 kg. pressure and cook for required time.

4 Reduce pressure at room temperature. Remove muslin bag, add warmed sugar.

5 Return open cooker to stove, stir over low heat until

Preparing fruit for grapefruit marmalade

Adding water to fruit in pressure cooker

Filling jars with a ladle

sugar has dissolved, then boil rapidly until setting point is reached (see page 8). This will take about 10 minutes.

The marmalade should be allowed to stand in the cooker until a skin forms. This will prevent the fruit rising in the jars. Fill clean, dry, warm jars to the very top. Cover immediately, or leave until quite cold and then cover.

Marmalade Ingredients
preparation and yield cooking at
10 lb./5 kg. pressure

Seville Orange
Yield approx 6½ lb./3 kg.

Imperial/Metric	American
2 lb./1 kg. Seville oranges	2 lb. Seville (bitter) oranges
2 pints/generous litre water	5 cups water
4 lb./2 kg. sugar	4 lb. sugar
juice of 2 lemons	juice of 2 lemons

Follow steps 1–5. Add lemon juice with sugar.

Lemon
Yield approx 4 lb./2 kg.

Imperial/Metric	American
1 lb./½ kg. lemons	1 lb. lemons
1 pint/6 dl. water	2½ cups water
2½ lb./1¼ kg. sugar	2½ lb. sugar

Follow steps 1–5.

Grapefruit
Yield approx 5 lb./2¼ kg.

Imperial/Metric	American
2 grapefruit	2 grapefruit
4 lemons	4 lemons
1½ pints/scant litre water	3¾ cups water
3 lb./1 kg. 400 g. sugar	3 lb. sugar

Follow steps 1–5.

Three-Fruit
Yield approx 6½ lb./3 kg.

Imperial/Metric	American
2 oranges	2 oranges
1 grapefruit	1 grapefruit
2 lemons	2 lemons
(making approx. 2 lb./1 kg. fruit)	(making approx. 2 lb. fruit)
1½ pints/ scant litre water	3¾ cups water
4 lb./2 kg. sugar	4 lb. sugar

Cut fruit in quarters. Remove trivet, put in water and fruit. Continue as in step 3. Reduce pressure at room temperature. Strain fruit. Chop according to taste. Remove all pips. Return fruit and juice to cooker. Add warmed sugar. Follow step 5.

Jelly marmalade, see recipe, page 24

Fruit Preserving and Syrups: Vegetable Preserving

The two essentials for successful fruit preserving are thoroughly sterilised fruit and perfectly sealed jars. You will waste time and money if you do not make sure on these two points, for in a very short time you will have a lot of unusable fruit on your hands.

First of all see that your jars, and especially the lids, are sound. In the newest type of jars, the glass lid and rubber band has been replaced by a lacquered metal disc with rubber band attached; this is easier to fit and there is no risk of the rubber band slipping during fixing and sterilisation. The usual screwband is still used to secure the disc. The necks of these jars are wide enough for the hand to be put in to arrange the fruit – a great time-saver and the most certain way of making sure that the jars are well packed so that there are no apertures among the fruit to cause sinking during sterilisation, and so leaving an empty space at the top of the jar. The jars are 'all-purpose' – they can be used for preserves, pickles and chutneys, as well as for bottling, and several sizes are available. If you are using the old-style glass tops with rubber bands, be sure that the glass tops are unchipped and the rubber rings soft and elastic. To be on the safe side, new rubber rings should be bought each season. Scald rubber rings, tops and screwbands, and thoroughly wash and rinse out jars with boiling water before use. It is better not to dry the jars.

Fruit for preserving should be ripe, but firm and unbruised. Gooseberries are an exception – they are usually bottled when green and under-ripe. Most plums should be firm-ripe, but greengages are better just before they are quite ripe. Apples and pears that are slightly bruised can be used, but all the bruised parts must be cut away. Fruit should be graded for size to ensure even cooking and to give a better appearance. (This is very important if you are thinking of showing bottled fruit at a garden or horticultural show.) You can bottle in plain boiled water, but the fruit will have a better flavour if a syrup is used. No amount of sugar added at the moment of eating seems to give the same flavour, or to really sweeten fruit bottled in water. Don't use too heavy a syrup; it causes the fruit to rise in the jars and is really unnecessary; 4–6 oz. of sugar to 1 pint of water (125–175 g. to 6 dl., $\frac{1}{2}$–$\frac{3}{4}$ cup to $2\frac{1}{2}$ cups) makes a good *light syrup*, but you can increase it according to taste. Boil the sugar and water together for a minute or two, then strain it through a nylon sieve or muslin. The syrup is used cold for both the water bath and oven methods of sterilisation.

Water bath method
You need a vessel deep enough to allow the jars to be completely covered with water – a deep saucepan, fish kettle, zinc pail, or washing boiler. Proper sterilisers with thermometers and rack attached can be bought, and if you are bottling large quantities it is worthwhile investing in one. With other vessels a false bottom must

be improvised – wooden slats, or a grid – so that the jars do not come in direct contact with the bottom of the pan. Jars must not be allowed to touch each other in the pan, so put a piece of cardboard between each.

Carefully pack the prepared fruit into the scalded jars, grading it for size as you go. Fill the jars just to the tops without crushing, then pour in cold syrup, allowing time for it to seep right through the fruit. Make sure there are no air bubbles. Fix on the tops and screwbands tightly, then give the bands one half-turn to loosen them. This is most important; if the bands should be too tight during sterilising the contents of bottles might expand, and air, not being able to escape, would burst the jars.

Arrange the jars in the water bath, cover with cold water, put cover on pan, and place on the cooker at its lowest heat, then bring the water to simmering point. It should take $1\frac{1}{2}$ hours for the water to reach this heat – $175°F./80°C.$

The water bath is held at simmering point for 10–15 minutes, according to the size and type of fruit. Very large fruit, such as whole pears, apples and peaches, Victoria plums, should be brought to $190°F./88°C.$, (water will show a definite ripple) and held there for 15 minutes.

Take the jars out of the water, one at a time, on to a wooden table or board, and tighten the screwband on each one immediately.

The oven method
Fill the jars as for the water bath method. Pour water in a baking tin to a depth of 1 inch/$2\frac{1}{2}$ cm., and stand the heated jars in the tin. Then place in the oven (275–300°F., 140–150°C., Gas Mark 1–2) and hold at that temperature for 1–$1\frac{1}{2}$ hours. Tighten the screwbands before removing the tray from the oven, then place on wooden table or board to cool, tightening the screwbands from time to time.

Bottling by pressure cooker
Fruit can be bottled very quickly in a pressure cooker with variable pressures – that is, 5 lb., 10 lb., or 15 lb. ($2\frac{1}{2}$, 5 or $7\frac{1}{2}$ kg.). Though the preparation of the fruit is the same as for the water bath or oven methods, the instructions given for sterilising by your own particular make of cooker must be most carefully followed, and the time-table strictly kept to. The times given are so short that there is a temptation to give just a minute longer, but that minute can be fatal, the fruit being hopelessly over-cooked.

Testing for seal
The day after bottling, take off the screwbands and lift each jar by its lid. The seal of every jar that can be lifted in this way should be perfect; if, however, the lid comes off, the fruit should be eaten within a few days.

Or if you wish to re-seal, find out the cause of failure to form a vacuum (i.e. whether contents have not reached boiling point, or rubber bands are not correctly placed) and re-process at once.

Storing
Light spoils the colour of the fruit and clouds the syrup, so store jars in a cool, dark place. Label each one with date of bottling so you know which should be used first. Although perfectly sterilised fruit will keep for months, sometimes years, it is well to examine the jars from time to time, since there are still many unknown causes of fermentation in fruit, and if you see any sign of trouble use the fruit immediately.

Bottled blackcurrants, redcurrants and soft berry fruits
When bottling currants – red or black – or soft berries such as raspberries, blackberries or loganberries, it is impossible to judge exactly how much fruit or syrup will be required to fill the jars; the quantity of fruit depends on the size of the fruits, how closely they can be packed into the jars without crushing them, and the quantity of liquid depends on the closeness of the pack. You can only fill up the jars almost to the top with the prepared berries, and have enough cold syrup ready to fill the jars to the brim. Roughly speaking, $1\frac{1}{2}$ pints (9 dl., $3\frac{3}{4}$ cups) of syrup (see page 28) will be sufficient to fill three 1-lb./450-g. jars of fruit.

It is best to always use small jars for bottling soft fruits; you can be more sure of complete sterilisation right through to the centre of the jars without any over-cooking of the berries. Large jars need longer sterilisation, and break-down of the berries may result.

Blackcurrants
Remove the stalks, using sharp scissors; it is not necessary to remove the brown blossom ends. Wipe the currants gently in a dry cloth. Pack into sterilised jars, shaking them down; jars should be closely packed without crushing the currants. Fill to $\frac{1}{2}$ inch/1 cm. from the top of the jars, then fill to brim with syrup (see page 28), put on covers and screwbands. Sterilise as instructed on page 28, taking $1\frac{1}{2}$ hours to reach $180°F./82°C.$ on the thermometer, and holding at this temperature 15 minutes.

Redcurrants
Only large varieties should be bottled; small currants are apt to shrink, and while the juice is red, the currants themselves become an insipid pink. It is really best to combine redcurrants with raspberries or loganberries, when more colour is retained; they are also excellent mixed with red cherries, improving the flavour of the cherries.

Blackberries
These are especially worthwhile bottling if you have access to plump wild ones, but they are still very good if

cultivated berries are used. A few jars of blackberries will go very well with fresh or bottled apples for a delicious winter-time blackberry and apple pie. Use fully ripe, but dry, uncrushed berries, pick them over for stray leaves, etc., wipe gently, and proceed as for blackcurrants.

Raspberries

Raspberries bruise very easily and should be gathered when just firm-ripe and handled as little as possible. When you grow your own it is a good idea to take the thoroughly cleaned jars to the raspberry canes and put the berries straight into the jars. Then, when you are ready to sterilise them, pour cold, boiled water from the kettle over the berries in the jars, invert the jars with your hand over the top, and strain away the water. This is sufficient to remove any 'foreign bodies'.

Fill up the jars with a light syrup (see page 28), put on lids and screwbands, and sterilise as described on page 28, taking $1\frac{1}{2}$ hours to reach simmering point or $168°F./75°C.$, and hold at this temperature for 10 minutes.

Raspberries can be bottled without syrup; just sprinkle castor sugar over the rinsed berries in the jars, allowing about $1\frac{1}{2}$ tablespoons for a small jar, put on lids and screwbands, and sterilise as for raspberries in syrup. The berries will sink in the jars, but they are delicious, being bottled in their own juice.

Loganberries

Loganberries are bottled in the same way as raspberries, but they need extra care and inspection in preparation, as they contain more grubs than any other fruit. To make sure you have removed all of these little pests, the berries should be put in a solution of salt water ($\frac{1}{2}$ oz./ 15 g. salt to 2 pints (1 litre, 5 cups) water), well rinsed in cold water, and drained before putting into the jars.

Strawberries

Strawberries *can* be bottled in the same way as raspberries, but they lose colour badly. It helps if a few redcurrants are mixed with them, or redcurrant juice used instead of plain syrup.

Preserved (Bottled) Cherries

Yield approx 2 1-lb./$\frac{1}{2}$-kg. jars

Imperial/Metric	American
$1\frac{1}{2}$–2 lb./$\frac{3}{4}$–1 kg. red or black sweet cherries	$1\frac{1}{2}$–2 lb. red or black sweet cherries
1–$1\frac{1}{2}$ pints/6–9 dl. light syrup (see page 28)	$2\frac{1}{2}$–$3\frac{3}{4}$ cups light syrup (see page 28)

Best cherries for bottling are Napoleons, Early Rivers or the old-fashioned black cherries sometimes called Blackhearts. Whitehearts are really not very good for bottling; although they look good in the jars, they are rather tasteless.

The cherries may be stoned if you have time and patience to do it, but here again, they have better flavour if the stones are kept in. There are cherry stoners available, but the job can be done with a sharp-pointed knife, cutting the cherries halfway round and twisting out the stone with the knife point. Whatever method you use, be sure to catch all the juice and add it to the jars.

Some of the stone kernels should be added to the jars, as they give a distinctive flavour to the fruit – almost kirsch-like. This flavour can be caught still more if you crack the stones (put them in a cloth and bang them with a hammer), cover with water and boil them. Strain and add the liquid to the water when making the syrup. Pack the cherries in sterilised jars, adding kernels to each jar, fill to the brim with syrup, then put on lids and screwbands loosely. Proceed as described in general instructions for water bath or oven method (see page 28), taking $1\frac{1}{2}$ hours to reach simmering point and holding at this temperature for 10 minutes.

Pear sections in almond syrup, see recipe, page 34
Making mincemeat, see recipe, page 20

Preserved (Bottled) Apricots

Yield approx 2 1-lb./½-kg. jars

Imperial/Metric	American
1½ lb./¾ kg. fresh apricots	1½ lb. fresh apricots
1–1½ pints/6–9 dl. light syrup (see page 28)	2½–3¾ cups light syrup (see page 28)

Apricots should be firm-ripe, without bruises. Under-ripe apricots have little juice and are apt to be tasteless. If the apricots are on the small side, they are best unstoned. I think they taste better this way, but if large, they can be stoned. Halved and stoned apricots are easier to pack closely in the jars. To stone, insert a pointed, stainless knife at the stalk-end and cut through to the stone right round. Then gently twist the two halves in opposite directions; if fully ripe the stones will be quite loose and ready to drop out. Crack a few of the stones and skin the kernels.

Closely pack the apricots in sterilised jars; if whole, it is better to arrange them in layers. Add a few kernels to each jar if fruit is halved. Fill up to tops of jars with light syrup, and proceed as described in general bottling directions for water or oven methods (see page 28), taking 1½ hours to reach simmering point and holding at this temperature for 10 minutes. Halved apricots take as long to sterilise as whole ones as they make a more solid pack in the jars, and time must be allowed for heat to penetrate to centre.

Peaches

Peaches are treated in the same way as apricots for bottling in syrup, but as they are larger, it is usual to halve or quarter them. They should be skinned; if just ripe the skinning can be done by peeling the quarters downwards from the stalk ends after removing stones. Slightly under-ripe fruit should be put in boiling water for a few seconds so that the skins can be rubbed off with a soft cloth, or peeled off with a knife.

Sliced peaches

Sliced peaches are very attractive and to my mind more useful than halved or quartered fruit; they can be added to fruit salads or used in flans. The peaches are easily arranged in circles of overlapping slices in the flan case; the syrup should be thickened slightly with cornflour, just brought to the boil and cooled, then poured over the peaches in the pastry case.

Preserved (Bottled) Apples or Pears
in light syrup

Yield approx 2 1-lb./½-kg. jars

Imperial/Metric	American
1½–2 lb./¾–1 kg. dessert apples or pears	1½–2 lb. dessert apples or pears
½ oz./15 g. salt	2 teaspoons salt
2 pints/generous litre cold water	5 cups cold water
juice of 1 lemon	juice of 1 lemon
1½ pints/9 dl. light syrup (see page 28)	3¾ cups light syrup (see page 28)

Peel the apples or pears, quarter them, and remove cores. As each is peeled, drop the sections into a brine solution, made by dissolving the salt in the water and lemon juice. Apples and pears discolour very quickly when exposed to the air; the solution keeps them white. Put a plate in the basin so that it is resting on the fruit. This keeps the fruit submerged until all has been prepared.

Have sterilised jars and covers ready. Rinse the fruit under running cold water; drain well. Pack the sections of fruit in 1 lb./½ kg. jars, taking care not to leave any spaces; with wide-necked jars this is easy to do with your hand, but with the narrow-necked jars, use a wooden spoon handle to pack the fruit. Be careful not to bruise it; pears particularly bruise very easily.

Fill jars to overflowing with the cold syrup, put on covers and screwbands. Stand the jars in a water bath, and follow the general instructions for sterilising at 175–190°F./80–88°C. (see page 28), taking 1½ hours to reach simmering point. Maintain this 10 minutes for apples and 20 minutes for pears. Remove from the water and tighten screwbands at once; while fruit is cooling you will need to tighten the bands further from time to time. Test for a good seal the following day (see page 29).

Bottled Gooseberries

Gooseberries for bottling should be on the under-ripe side, though not so hard that they are lacking in juice. As the gooseberries get riper their skins get tougher, so it is best to use berries that are just on the 'turn'.

Wash, top and tail the berries. As you snip off the stalk ends, try to cut away a scrap of the skin; this prevents the skins bursting during sterilisation, and allows the syrup to penetrate into the fruit.

It is best to grade the fruit for size as you put it into the sterilised jars; not only does this look better but it means that the berries are evenly cooked. (If you think of entering any bottled fruit at the local produce show, this grading for size is a winning point.)

Fill up the jars to overflowing with light syrup (see page 28), put on lids and screwbands and sterilise according to general instructions for water bath or oven method (see page 28), allowing $1\frac{1}{2}$ hours to reach simmering point and maintaining this for 10 minutes.

Remove from water or oven, tighten screwbands, and leave to cool, giving the screwbands a twist, two or three times during cooling. Test for a good seal next day (see page 29).

Bottled Tomatoes

Choose firm, sound tomatoes, no bigger than a golf ball, if possible, as these can be bottled whole. After skinning, pack the tomatoes tightly in sterilised jars, cutting them if necessary (whole and cut tomatoes should not be packed in the same jar); sprinkle with $\frac{1}{2}$ teaspoon sugar and 1 teaspoon of salt to each 1 lb./$\frac{1}{2}$ kg. of tomatoes. Do not add any water. Cover jars either with the lacquered metal/rubber discs or with sterilised rubber rings and glass caps, put on screwbands, giving bands a half-turn back. Immerse jars in cold water, and bring up to simmering point slowly, taking 1 hour. Hold at this temperature for 30 minutes, then tighten screwbands, remove jars, and leave them to cool, tightening the bands from time to time.

Bottled Fruit Salad

Yield approx 2-lb./1-kg. screw-top fruit jar

Imperial/Metric	American
4 oz./125 g. black cherries	$\frac{3}{4}$ cup bing cherries
4 oz./125 g. loganberries	1 cup loganberries
4 oz./125 g. blackcurrants	1 cup black currants
4 oz./125 g. redcurrants	1 cup red currants
6 oz./175 g. strawberries	$1\frac{1}{3}$ cups strawberries
6 oz./175 g. raspberries	$1\frac{1}{3}$ cups raspberries
4 heaped teaspoons castor sugar	4 heaped teaspoons sugar
4 pints/$2\frac{1}{4}$ litres boiled water	5 pints boiled water

Wash the fruit jar, rubber band, glass top and screwband, and rinse with boiling water. Do not dry jar; keep the rubber band and lid in boiled water while filling jar.

Pick over the fruit, removing stalks and any that is damaged. Avoid washing it, but wipe on a damp towel. Halve cherries and stone over a basin to catch any juice that is squeezed out. Put cherries in bottom of the jar; sprinkle with 1 teaspoon of sugar; next put in the loganberries then the blackcurrants, followed by the redcurrants, sprinkling a spoonful of sugar between each layer. Shake the jar from time to time so that the fruit packs closely. Put in the strawberries, and lastly the

raspberries; no sugar is needed for these. Pour in the boiled water (hot but not boiling), then put on rubber ring and glass top. Fix on the screwband tightly, then give it one half-turn backwards.

Stand jar in deep pan on thick cardboard to prevent cracking. Fill pan with enough water to come right over the shoulder of the jar, place over a low burner and bring to simmering point very slowly, taking $1-1\frac{1}{2}$ hours. Hold at simmering point for 5 minutes, then take the jar on to a wooden table, tighten screwband, and leave to cool. Twist the band from time to time while jar is cooling to make sure it is quite tight. Being soft, the fruit may sink a little in the jar.

Preserved Honey Fruit Compote

Yield approx 4–5 1-lb./$\frac{1}{2}$-kg. jars

Imperial/Metric	American
8 oz./225 g. dried prunes	$1\frac{1}{3}$ cups dried prunes
8 oz./225 g. dried apricots	$1\frac{1}{3}$ cups dried apricots
8 oz./225 g. dried figs	$1\frac{1}{3}$ cups dried figs
8 oz./225 g. dried peaches	$1\frac{1}{3}$ cups dried peaches
2 pints/generous litre water	5 cups water
10 oz./275 g. clear Australian honey	$\frac{3}{4}$ cup clear honey
thinly pared rind of 1 lemon	thinly pared rind of 1 lemon

Soak dried fruits in the water overnight. Drain, reserving water.

Dissolve the honey in the reserved water and boil, together with the rind, for 5 minutes. Remove the rind. Pack the fruit into sterilised preserving jars. Cover with syrup to within $\frac{1}{2}$ inch/$1\frac{1}{4}$ cm. of the top of the jars, adding a little more water, if necessary. Stand the jars on a rack in a deep preserving pan and add warm water to come level with the necks of the jars.

Bring slowly to the boil and simmer for 3 minutes. Cover with the lids and screw down loosely. Continue simmering for 25 minutes. Tighten screwbands, and remove jars.

Pear Sections in Almond Syrup

Yield approx 4–5 1-lb./½-kg. jars

Imperial/Metric	American
2 pints/generous litre water	5 cups water
juice of 2 lemons	juice of 2 lemons
3½ lb./1¾ kg. sugar	3½ lb. sugar
12 oz./350 g. blanched almonds	12 oz. (3 cups) blanched almonds
little colouring	little coloring
4 lb./2 kg. dessert pears, peeled, cored and cut into sections	4 lb. dessert pears, pared, cored and cut into sections

Bring the water to the boil, together with the lemon juice, sugar, 8 oz. (225 g., 2 cups) of the almonds and a little colouring, and continue boiling until the syrup thickens. Add the pear sections to the remaining almonds, place in the syrup and bring to the boil. Simmer 1–2 minutes. Immediately turn into hot sterilised preserving jars, and seal.

It is unnecessary to cook the pears until tender, as it is essential that they keep their shape and contrast in colour to the liquid. The syrup acts as a preservative if jars are sealed at boiling point. Heat through to serve.

Shown in colour on page 31

Pear Preserves

Yield approx 3 1-lb./½-kg. jars

Imperial/Metric	American
2 lb./1 kg. granulated sugar	2 lb. sugar
1¼ pints/7½ dl. water	3 cups water
4 tablespoons honey	5 tablespoons honey
2 lb./1 kg. pears, peeled, cored and cut in halves	2 lb. pears, pared, cored and cut in halves
8 whole cloves	8 whole cloves
1 oz./25 g. raisins	2 tablespoons raisins
1 lemon, thinly sliced	1 lemon, thinly sliced

Dissolve the sugar in the water, over gentle heat. Add the honey and boil rapidly for 8 minutes. Put the pear halves, cloves, raisins and lemon slices into the syrup. Cook until the pears are tender and the syrup is thick. Spoon the pears into hot, sterilised preserving jars. Top up with syrup and seal, either by water bath or oven sterilising method.

Preserved (Bottled) Fruit Pulp

It is a good idea to pulp fruit such as apples and tomatoes when there is a glut of them; you get a lot of fruit in a small space by this method. It is an excellent way of using up windfall apples and those small tomatoes often sold very cheaply as 'thinnings'. Apple pulp is very useful for making puddings, apple sauce, and as an alternative to jam in sponge sandwich cakes. Tomato pulp added to well seasoned stock makes a quick tomato soup; used as it is, seasoned with spicy bottled sauce, you have an instant tomato sauce. Useful for seasoning stews and casseroles too.

Preserved apple pulp

Windfalls or damaged apples can be used in this way, but choose apples that 'fall' quickly in cooking, and are white and fluffy. Apples can be pulped without sugar, but even a little sugar gives an improvement in flavour, and helps to preserve the fruit. Peel, core and cut up fruit roughly, removing all bruises and damaged parts. Stew the fruit in enough water to float it, adding a little sugar. Stir often until boiling, then simmer until soft. Beat with a whisk until light and fluffy. While still boiling, pour into hot, sterilised jars. Put on covers. Stand jars in water slightly below boiling point, bring to the boil, and keep at this temperature for 5 minutes. Then remove, tighten screwbands, cool and test the jars as for bottled fruit.

Tomato pulp

Choose perfectly ripe, but not soft tomatoes. Wash, cut up and put into a pan with ½ tablespoon salt to each 2 lb./1 kg. tomatoes. Bring to the boil, stirring often, and simmer until pulpy. Sieve, return to saucepan and bring to boiling point again. Pour into hot, sterilised jars, cover, and place in pan with enough hot water to cover the jars. Bring to simmering point and keep at this temperature for 15 minutes. Remove from heat, tighten screwbands, cool and test as for fruits.

Syrups

If you have a store of concentrated syrups in your larder you will be able to produce quickly any favourite sauce for serving with ice creams or other sweets. You will also have a constant supply of instant delicious drinks for the family, topping up the glass with milk.

Fruit Syrups

Pressing out the juice

Always use fully ripe, soft fruits for syrups. Put the fruit into an earthenware bowl over a pan of hot water. In the case of red-, white- or blackcurrants, 1 pint (6 dl., 2½ cups) of water may be added to 2 lb./1 kg. of fruit. Other soft fruits do not require water.
Crush the fruit with a wooden spoon or masher. Allow to drip through four thicknesses of butter-muslin – either overnight or for about 8 hours. Squeeze the remaining juice through the cloth, twisting the ends in opposite directions.

Addition of Sugar

Measure the juice and add 12 oz./350 g. of sugar per 1 pint (6 dl., 2½ cups) of juice, heat gently, stir until the sugar is dissolved. Fill sterilised bottles to within 2 inches (5 cm.) of the top. Stopper with corks that have been boiled for 15 minutes immediately before use. Secure the corks firmly with wire or tie them down with string to prevent their being forced out during heating.

Sterilise by gradually raising the temperature to 170°F./77°C.; maintain this temperature for 30 minutes. Drive the corks home and remove the strings. Store in a cool, dark place.

Syrup for Sauces
basic recipe

Imperial/Metric	American
1 lb./450 g. lump sugar	*1 lb. sugar, preferably cube*
1 pint/6 dl. water	*2½ cups water*

Dissolve the sugar in the water over heat, and skim the surface. Boil to 220°F./110°C. (measure with a sugar thermometer), then allow to cool. When cold, store in bottles.

This basic syrup may be flavoured by adding any type of essence or spice. In addition, some variations using the basic syrup are described below.

Syrup Sauce Variations

Almond Syrup

Imperial/Metric	American
8 oz./225 g. sweet almonds	*½ lb. (2 cups) sweet almonds*
1 oz./25 g. bitter almonds	*1 oz. (¼ cup) bitter almonds*
1 pint/6 dl. basic syrup	*2½ cups basic syrup*

Shell and skin the almonds and pound to a paste. Gradually add the basic syrup to the paste. Reheat gently and allow to cool, then strain.

Baba Syrup

Imperial/Metric	American
rinds of 1 orange and 1 lemon	*rinds of 1 orange and 1 lemon*
1 pint/6 dl. basic syrup	*2½ cups basic syrup*
¼ pint/1½ dl. rum	*⅔ cup rum*

Add the rinds of orange and lemon to the syrup. Boil for 2 minutes, then allow to cool. Strain and add the rum.

Blackcurrant Syrup
imitation cassis

Imperial/Metric	American
1 lb./½ kg. blackcurrants	*1 lb. black currants*
1 pint/6 dl. basic syrup	*2½ cups basic syrup*

Add the blackcurrants to the basic syrup and boil for 5 minutes. Allow to cool and then strain. A tablespoon of 'cassis' added to a glass of white wine with a dash of brandy makes a delicious drink.

Chocolate Syrup

Imperial/Metric	American
8 oz./225 g. chocolate	*½ lb. chocolate*
1 pint/6 dl. basic syrup	*2½ cups basic syrup*

Melt the chocolate in a basin over a saucepan of hot water. Gradually stir in the syrup. Blend well.

Cranberry Syrup

Imperial/Metric	American
1 lb./½ kg. cranberries	*1 lb. cranberries*
1 pint/6 dl. basic syrup	*2½ cups basic syrup*
4 tablespoons port wine	*⅓ cup port wine*
4 tablespoons redcurrant jelly	*⅓ cup red currant jelly*

Add the fruit to the syrup and boil for 5 minutes. Then add the port wine and the redcurrant jelly. Allow to cool, then strain.

Ginger Syrup

Imperial/Metric	American
¼ oz./8 g. stick ginger root	*¼ oz. ginger root*
juice of 1 lemon	*juice of 1 lemon*
1 pint/6 dl. basic syrup	*2½ cups basic syrup*

Add the ginger and lemon juice to the syrup and boil for 5 minutes. Allow to cool. Strain.

Lemon Syrup

Imperial/Metric	American
6 lemons	*6 lemons*
1 pint/6 dl. basic syrup	*2½ cups basic syrup*

Soak rind and juice of the lemons in the syrup overnight. Next day, boil for 5 minutes, cool and strain.

Maple Syrup

Imperial/Metric	American
1 lb./450 g. maple sugar	1 lb. maple sugar
1 pint/6 dl. water	2½ cups water

Boil the sugar and water together to 220°F./110°C. (measure with a sugar thermometer). Remove any scum from the surface. Allow to cool. Strain.

Pineapple Syrup

Imperial/Metric	American
1 lb./½ kg. fresh pineapple cubes	1 lb. fresh pineapple cubes
1 pint/6 dl. water	2½ cups water
1 lb./½ kg. sugar	1 lb. sugar
pinch of saffron	pinch of saffron

Boil all ingredients together, except saffron, to 220°F./110°C. (using a sugar thermometer to measure) Remove any scum. Add the saffron colouring. Allow to cool. Strain. The pineapple can be used as a sweet.

Trifle Syrup

Imperial/Metric	American
rind and juice of 1 lemon	rind and juice of 1 lemon
small stick of cinnamon	small stick of cinnamon
few caraway seeds	few caraway seeds
1 pint/6 dl. basic syrup	2½ cups basic syrup

Add the lemon rind and juice, the cinnamon and the caraway seeds to the syrup. Boil together for 5 minutes. Cover the saucepan with a lid, allow to cool and strain.

Apple Syrup

Yield approx 4 pints/2¼ litres/5 pints

Imperial/Metric	American
12 lb./5¾ kg. ripe, juicy cooking apples	12 lb. ripe, juicy cooking apples
8 oz./225 g. lump sugar per 1 pint/6 dl. of juice	½ lb. cube sugar per 2½ cups of juice
4 cloves	4 cloves
2-inch/5-cm. stick of cinnamon	2-inch stick of cinnamon

Wipe apples with damp cloth, do not peel or core. Slice or cut up roughly, removing any bruised or unsound parts; as cut, drop into bowl of salted water to prevent discoloration – 1½ oz./40 g. salt to 1 gallon (4½ litres, 10 pints) water. Drain about two-thirds of the apples, put into preserving pan and barely cover with water. Bring to boil, and continue boiling gently until fruit is partially broken down. Now drain carefully, and put rest of apples into the juice. Bring back to the boil, simmer for 1 hour. Strain through a jelly bag, leave to drip overnight.

Measure juice; weigh required amount of sugar. Put juice in clean pan, boil for 15 minutes; remove pan from heat, add warm sugar, cloves, and cinnamon. Stir until sugar is melted, return pan to heat, bring to boil again, then boil gently for 30 minutes. Skim. Remove spices. Allow to cool. Pour into warm jars and sterilise as explained under bottling directions (see page 28).

Blackcurrant Syrup

Put the cleaned blackcurrants in a casserole or stew-jar, with a little water to float them. Stand the jar in a cool oven until blackcurrants are soft, then crush them with a wooden spoon and strain through a nylon sieve.

Measure juice and add 12 oz./350 g. sugar to each 1 pint (6 dl., 2½ cups). Boil juice and sugar until slightly thickened, pour into screw-top bottles, cork loosely and stand bottles in a pan with water up to the shoulders of the bottles. Bring slowly to boiling point and keep at this temperature for 5 minutes. Remove bottles, push in corks immediately then put on screw caps. The corks should come level to top of bottles.

Elderberry Syrup

Yield approx 2 pints/1 litre/2½ pints

Imperial/Metric	American
4½ lb./2 kg. ripe elderberries	4½ lb. ripe elderberries
1 lb./½ kg. ripe, juicy cooking apples	1 lb. ripe, juicy cooking apples
1¾ pints/1 litre water	4¼ cups water
6 oz./175 g. lump sugar per 1 pint/6 dl. of juice	6 oz. cube sugar per 2½ cups of juice
4 cloves	4 cloves
3-inch/7½-cm. stick of cinnamon	3-inch stick of cinnamon

Pick over and wash elderberries; wipe apples, do not peel or core, cut up small, removing any blemished parts. Put apples in preserving pan with the water, boil gently until reduced to a pulp; add elderberries, return to boil, then simmer to extract and concentrate juice, about 45 minutes. Strain through a jelly bag, leaving to drip overnight.

Measure juice, weigh out required amount of sugar. Put juice in a clean pan, heat without boiling, add warmed sugar and spices, stir until sugar is melted, then boil gently for 30 minutes. Skim, and remove spices. Bottle and sterilise (see page 28).

Blackberry Syrup

Yield approx 2 pints/1¼ litres/2½ pints

Imperial/Metric	American
4–5 lb./1¾–2¼ kg. ripe blackberries	4–5 lb. ripe blackberries
6 oz./175 g. lump sugar per 1 pint/6 dl. of juice	6 oz. cube sugar per 2½ cups of juice

Pick over and wash blackberries. Put in preserving pan with 1 pint (6 dl., 2½ cups) water; bring to boil, then simmer to extract juice, about 45 minutes. Strain through a jelly bag, leaving to drip overnight.

Measure juice; weigh out required amount of sugar then put in slow oven to warm. Put juice in clean pan, boil gently for 10 minutes; remove pan to side of cooker, allow to go off the boil, then add warm sugar, stir until melted, return pan to heat. Boil gently for 20 minutes. Skim, bottle and sterilise (see page 28).

Strawberry Syrup

Yield approx ¾–1 pint/4½–6 dl./2–2½ cups

Imperial/Metric	American
1½ lb./¾ kg. strawberries	1½ lb. strawberries
1¼ lb./600 g. sugar	1¼ lb. sugar

Clean and thoroughly crush strawberries in a small pan, then add 1 lb./½ kg. sugar. Cover pan. Place over very low heat for 1 hour. Bring just to boiling point. Strain through a fine hair, or nylon, sieve – pressing well. Add remaining sugar to the resulting syrup. Bring very slowly back to boiling point. Bottle in clean, warm, dry bottles, cork securely and seal with screw tops. Sterilise and store in a cool, dry place.

Use as a drink, adding 3 tablespoons to a tumbler of hot or cold water, or make jelly by mixing ½ pint (3 dl., 1¼ cups) syrup with ½ pint (3 dl., 1¼ cups) water, and adding 1½ tablepoons powdered gelatine previously softened in a little extra heated syrup.

Vegetable Preserving by Pressure Cooker

With the exception of tomatoes (which are really a fruit anyway), it is not safe to bottle vegetables in the same way as fruits – that is, by the water bath or the oven method. Vegetables are non-acid foods, which means that they do not contain sufficient acid to stop bacterial action, and ordinary processes will not kill the bacteria that set up fermentation and food poison. But if you have a pressure cooker, it is possible to bottle vegetables.

Preparing beans for bottling

Bottling potatoes by pressure cooker

Every care must be taken that the vegetables are young, fresh and sound, and that they are scrupulously clean. Any speck of earth that gets into the jars can set up poison.

All vegetables must be blanched before they are bottled. Blanching is the immersing of prepared vegetables in boiling water for a certain time, and then straining and rinsing them in cold water. They are then packed in the jars and covered with a brine solution (made by dissolving 3 oz./75 g. coarse salt in 1 gallon (4½ litres, 10 pints) boiling water). Extra care should be taken to see that preserving jars are perfectly sound, and new rubber rings should be used. The vegetables should not be too tightly packed in the sterilised jars; but at the same time, there should be no air bubbles, so twist the jars from side to side, and bang lightly on a wooden table to 'settle' the vegetables while you are packing them. Always leave 1 inch/2½ cm. clear space at the top of the jars.

French or runner beans

Small, young French beans can be bottled whole, topped and tailed with the strings removed. Runner beans are topped and tailed, strings removed and cut into slices. Wash well in several changes of water. Blanch in boiling water for 5 minutes, then rinse in cold water. Pack into sterilised jars. Cover with hot brine solution (see page 40). Adjust rubber rings and lids at once, fix on screw tops loosely. Put 1½ pints (9 dl., 3¾ cups) boiling water in pressure cooker, and stand the jars on the inverted trivet, making sure that they do not touch each other, or the sides of the cooker, by putting pieces of cardboard between them. Add 1 tablespoon of vinegar to the water in the cooker to prevent it discolouring. Place lid on cooker, bring to the boil, and boil without pressure for 5 minutes. Then put on 10 lb./5 kg. pressure control. Lower heat when pressure point is reached, and keep at this point for 40 minutes. Turn off heat and allow pressure to reduce for 15 minutes. Remove jars, tightening the screwbands as you take each one out, and leave to get cold. Tighten the screwbands once or twice while jars are cooling. Test for a good seal (see page 29) after 24 hours.

New potatoes

Choose equal-sized medium potatoes. Wash them well, and scrape. Choose easy scrapers, so that the flesh underneath is not damaged. Wash thoroughly after scraping to be sure that no scraps of skin get into the jars. Blanch potatoes for 5 minutes, rinse and pack into sterilised jars. Proceed as for beans, but allow 50 minutes at 10 lb./5 kg. pressure.

Carrots

Small young carrots can be bottled whole, larger ones should be cut into slices or quarters. Remove tops well down the carrots to be sure there is no green stalk or earth left on; cut off roots. Wash well and scrape.

Blanch for 10 minutes, rinse in cold water, and pack into the jars. Sterilise in pressure cooker as for beans, but allowing 45 minutes at 10 lb./5 kg. pressure.

Peas

Use only young peas. Shell, wash and grade them for size. Blanch for 3 minutes, rinse under cold water and pack equal-sized peas in the jars. Fill up with hot brine, and proceed as for beans, allowing 50 minutes at 10 lb./5 kg. pressure.

Safety First

If there is any doubt about the goodness of bottled vegetables when the jars are opened – if they smell musty or if there is any appearance of mushiness or sliminess – throw them away WITHOUT TASTING. All bottled vegetables should be boiled for a minute or two before they are tasted, as a safeguard.

Pickles, Chutneys and Relishes

The making of pickles, chutneys, and bottled sauces is a most interesting and rewarding way to preserve fruit and vegetables. We all know how expensive these pickles and chutneys are to buy, and how often we find that their flavour is not quite to our liking – either they are over-spiced and too 'vinegary', or they have no distinctive flavour and the ingredients, especially in the case of pickled onions, mixed pickles or piccalilli, are tough rather than crisp. So why not make your own?

The ingredients in themselves are not expensive; if you have a garden you can grow many of them. And believe me, the time and trouble is nothing compared to the satisfaction of seeing those jars in the pantry, ready to cheer up many a sad-looking piece of cold meat, or to help you to bring variety and flavour to your cooking. A spoonful of fruity chutney added to the ordinary stew or casserole, gives it an intriguing flavour; try adding one or two chopped pickled cucumbers to a pork casserole; or two or three sliced pickled walnuts to a steak and kidney stew. Have you tried pickled cucumbers with hot fried fish and chips? It's a continental habit and many foreign cafés and restaurants in our large towns and cities keep it up. Pickled pears, plums and damsons are excellent accompaniments to all kinds of hot meats and poultry, and a change from the eternal apple sauce with pork and duck. When peaches are cheap it is worthwhile spicing them to serve as a special treat with roast poultry or game; spiced pears, too, can take the place of apple sauce with pork.

In pickling it is important that everything should be the best and soundest obtainable; if you have to buy your fruits and vegetables, see that they are firm and not over-ripe, or, after a rainy summer, that they are not squishy through many soakings. Mis-shapen apples and pears can be used, windfalls too, so long as you are careful to cut out all bruised parts. But over-blown cauliflowers are not worth pickling, while knocked-about cucumbers and marrows can cause pickles and chutneys to go bad.

Vinegars

As vinegar is one of the most important ingredients in the making of pickles, chutneys and sauces it is worthwhile understanding a little about it. All genuine vinegars are produced by fermentation; alcohol in some form is turned into vinegar by the action of acetic acid but, while this acid is necessary to kill bacteria, yeasts and moulds, it is very important that there is not too much present in the vinegar, as this 'sours' it and has a bad effect on the ingredients to be pickled. There was a time, before the danger of this over-acidity was understood, when people would make their own vinegar (so-called, but as it was not brewed it could not be genuine) from acetic acid bought from the chemist, with water and gravy browning or caramel added. It was a harsh, fiery concoction and one hates to think what effect it would have on the food (or stomachs) coming in contact with it. This type of 'vinegar' is no longer sold in shops.

All genuine vinegars bought in bottles from reputable makers will make pickles, but malt and spirit vinegars are the best for strength, flavour and purity. Wine vinegar and distilled vinegar have delicate flavours which, while unbeatable for fine sauces and salad dressings, are quite lost in pickles; they are dearer, too. Bottled vinegars are usually of higher strength than bulk vinegar sold from the cask.

Be generous with the vinegar when making pickles; the vegetables should be well covered. It is best not to fill the jars quite up to the top with solids; you'll find in time that the vegetables soak up more vinegar, so leave a little extra on the top to allow for this. There should be at least ½ inch/1 cm. vinegar covering the top of the solids.

Pickling spices

In most cases vinegar is spiced for making pickles; not only does this give flavour to the pickle, but spices help in preservation. Bought, ready-mixed pickling spice can be used, but you can buy spices separately and blend them according to your taste (see this page). But never, never attempt to make pickles with unboiled vinegar – it will go sour on you in no time.

Salt

Salt is another important ingredient when pickling vegetables. There is a high proportion of water in most vegetables and as much of this as possible must be extracted by brine before vinegar is added. Not only does the salt draw out excess fluid from the vegetables, it firms them up so that you get a clearer pickle. Coarse, unrefined, block salt, or sea salt, should be used – not refined table salt which contains additives.

Equipment

Use earthenware bowls and enamel or heavy aluminium pans for pickling; never brass, copper or tin. Wooden spoons should be used for stirring and mixing. Glass or stone jars are best for potting, and they should not have metal lids that could come into contact with the pickle. Ordinary jam jars are suitable, covered with two layers of greaseproof or waxed paper and then with aluminium foil, tied on securely. Cork or plastic-lined clip-on lids may be used so long as no metal touches the pickle.

Storing

Uncooked pickles, such as pickled onions, clear mixed pickles, pickled cabbage, should be kept for a while before using – say 4–6 weeks – so they can absorb the spiced vinegar and be more tender. A cooked pickle, such as piccalilli, sweet pickles or chutneys can be eaten within a few days.

Standard Wet Brine for Pickles

Imperial/Metric	American
8 oz./225 g. coarse salt to 3 pints/1½ litres water	*½ lb. coarse pickling salt to 7½ cups water*

Bring to the boil and leave to go cold before using. Allow 1 pint (6 dl., 2½ cups) of brine to 1 lb./½ kg. vegetables.

Dry Brine

Slice or cut up the vegetables and place in layers on a shallow dish with a sprinkling of coarse salt between each layer.

This is a strong brine, too salty for some; the vegetables should be well drained of salt that has liquefied.

Standard Spiced Vinegar

Imperial/Metric	American
1 oz./25 g. peppercorns	*1 oz. peppercorns*
¼ oz./8 g. blade mace	*¼ oz. blade mace*
¼ oz./8 g. cloves	*¼ oz. cloves*
6 bay leaves	*6 bay leaves*
½ oz./15 g. bruised ginger root	*½ oz. bruised ginger root*
2 teaspoons mustard seeds	*2 teaspoons mustard seeds*
¼ oz./8 g. whole allspice	*¼ oz. whole allspice*
¼ oz./8 g. stick of cinnamon	*¼ oz. stick of cinnamon*
4 chillis, crushed	*4 chilis, crushed*
1 tablespoon salt	*1 tablespoon salt*
2 pints/generous litre malt vinegar	*5 cups malt vinegar*

Boil the spices and salt in a little of the vinegar for 1–2 minutes, to extract their flavour, then add remaining vinegar, boil for a further 3 minutes, strain and cool.

Ready-mixed pickling spice may be used, when 2 oz./50 g. to 2 pints (generous litre, 5 cups) vinegar will be required. It is doubtful if cinnamon and bay leaves will be included, so these will have to be added.

The spiced vinegar is used cold for crisp pickles, but if a soft pickle – for pickled onions, clear mixed pickles, pickled cucumbers – is preferred, then the vinegar should be used hot.

Note

Vinegar evaporates considerably when boiled, therefore it is a saving to boil the bulk of the vinegar no longer than 3 minutes.

Clear mixed pickles

Clear Mixed Pickles

Yield approx 4–5 lb./2 kg.

Imperial/Metric	American
1 lb./½ kg. shallots	1 lb. shallots
1 lb./½ kg. cauliflower	1 lb. cauliflower
large cucumber or 2 ridge cucumbers	large cucumber or 2 ridge cucumbers
2 tablespoons coarse salt	3 tablespoons pickling salt
3 pints/1½ litres spiced vinegar	7½ cups spiced vinegar
pickling spices, chillis	pickling spices, chilis

Peel the shallots, remove green from cauliflower and break into sprigs. Peel cucumber and cut into cubes. Place on a dish, sprinkle with salt and leave overnight. Strain off the salt and pack vegetables in layers in glass jars. Fill up with cold spiced vinegar, adding a few spices and chillis. Tie down.

Keep for a few months before using.

Pickled Cabbage

Yield approx 2½–3 lb./1¼–1½ kg.

Imperial/Metric	American
3 lb./1½ kg. red cabbage	3 lb. red cabbage
3–4 tablespoons coarse salt	4–5 tablespoons pickling salt
1–1½ pints/6–9 dl. cold spiced vinegar (see page 40)	2½–3¾ cups cold spiced vinegar (see page 40)

Remove outer leaves and stalk from cabbage, then wash and quarter it. Take out the hard centre stalk and shred the cabbage finely across the leaves. Spread cabbage on a shallow dish, sprinkling salt among the shreds. Put a final good layer of salt over the top, and leave overnight. Drain off liquid salt from cabbage by leaving it in a colander.

Pack, not too tightly, into glass jars; cover with the vinegar. Allow time for vinegar to seep through the cabbage, then top up until it reaches at least ½ inch/1 cm. above cabbage. It is best to leave jars overnight before the final topping up with vinegar. Tie down; keep at least 14 days before using.

Note
Ordinary jam jars are quite suitable to use for pickles, and plain white, or waxed paper, fastened down with string or rubber bands, can be used. Screwbands are not recommended, as it is important that vinegar should not come in contact with metal.

Shown in colour on page 55

Crisp Pickled Onions or Shallots

Yield approx 3–4 1-lb./½-kg. jars

Imperial/Metric	American
2 lb./1 kg. even sized onions or shallots	2 lb. even sized onions or shallots
2–3 tablespoons coarse salt	3–4 tablespoons pickling salt
2 pints/generous litre spiced vinegar (see page 40)	5 cups spiced vinegar (see page 40)

Peel the onions or shallots and spread on a shallow dish, sprinkling salt among them. Sprinkle a good layer of salt on top; leave overnight. Put the onions in a colander, rinse under cold water, leave to drain well. Pack them, not too tightly, into jars; arrange with the handle of a wooden spoon so there are no large spaces. Cover with cold spiced vinegar. Tie down. A few of the spices may be sprinkled on top.

Keep 3–4 weeks before using.

Sweet Pickled Onions

Yield approx 3–4 1-lb./½-kg. jars

Imperial/Metric	American
2 lb./1 kg. small onions or shallots	2 lb. small onions or shallots
4 pints/2¼ litres water	10 cups (5 pints) water
12 oz./350 g. coarse salt	1 cup pickling salt
2 pints/generous litre spiced vinegar (see page 40)	5 cups spiced vinegar (see page 40)
4 oz./125 g. Demerara sugar	½ cup raw sugar, firmly packed

Peel the onions or shallots, boil the water and salt, allow it to cool and pour half over the onions. Leave for 2 days, then drain onions and pour on remaining brine, leaving for 2 more days. Drain and rinse the onions, put into a pan with the spiced vinegar and the sugar and simmer for 10 minutes, put into jars and tie down when cold.

Keep for 2–3 weeks before using. This gives soft pickled onions.

Sweet Spiced Pickled Cucumber

Yield approx 4–5 lb./2 kg.

Imperial/Metric	American
6 large cucumbers (5 lb./2¼ kg.)	6 large cucumbers (5 lb.)
coarse salt	pickling salt
water	water
1 rounded teaspoon alum	1 rounded teaspoon alum
3 pints/1½ litres white malt vinegar	7½ cups white malt vinegar
3 lb./1½ kg. granulated sugar	3 lb. sugar
3 oz./75 g. mixed pickling spices	3 oz. mixed pickling spices
1-inch/2½-cm. stick cinnamon	1-inch stick cinnamon

Wash and wipe the cucumbers, halve them lengthwise, cut into 1-inch/2½-cm. thick slices and then into chunky pieces. Put into an earthenware bowl and cover with brine (2 oz./50 g. block salt to 1 pint/6 dl./2½ cups water) and add the alum. Cover and leave for 3 days. Drain and rinse well. Put into a pan with 1 pint (6 dl., 2½ cups) vinegar and a little water if necessary, to cover. Simmer until just tender and transparent-looking, about 30–40 minutes. Drain and put the cucumber into a large earthenware bowl.

Put the remaining 2 pints (1¼ litres, 2½ pints) of vinegar into a pan with sugar. Add the pickling spices and cinnamon tied in a piece of muslin. Bring to the boil for 5 minutes. Pour over the cucumber and leave to stand for 24 hours.

Next day, strain off the vinegar; bring it to the boil again and pour back over the cucumber. Leave for another 24 hours then repeat the straining, boiling up

and pouring back over the cucumber. Strain off the vinegar. Pack the cucumber into warm dry jars.

Boil up the vinegar without a lid until reduced by about one-third. Pour over the cucumber, cover and label when cold.

Pickled Ridge Cucumbers

Yield approx 2–3 1-lb./½-kg. jars

Imperial/Metric	American
2 lb./1 kg. outdoor (ridge) cucumbers	2 lb. outdoor (ridge) cucumbers
2 pints/1¼ litres water	5 cups water
6 oz./175 g. cooking salt	½ cup pickling salt
2 oz./50 g. granulated sugar	¼ cup sugar
2 pints/generous litre spiced vinegar (see page 40)	5 cups spiced vinegar (see page 40)
dried bay leaves	dried bay leaves

Choose young cucumbers with soft skins as they should not be peeled. Wipe them, halve, then quarter lengthwise. Boil water and salt together, allow to get cold. Put the cucumbers in this brine and leave for 24 hours. Dissolve sugar in spiced vinegar. Take cucumbers from brine. Rinse thoroughly in cold water, drain and leave for 1–2 hours to dry.

Pack upright in jars and fill up with cold spiced vinegar, to come at least ½ inch/1¼ cm. above top of cucumbers – use more vinegar, if necessary. Put a bay leaf on top of cucumbers in the jars. Seal securely and store in a cool place.

Ready to eat in 2–3 weeks.

My Special Piccalilli

Yield approx 12 lb./5½ kg.

Imperial/Metric	American
6 lb./3 kg. marrow, after preparation	6 lb. summer squash, after preparation
1 cucumber	1 cucumber
2 lb./1 kg. cauliflower	2 lb. cauliflower
2 lb./1 kg. shallots	2 lb. shallots
1 lb./½ kg. runner beans or French beans	1 lb. green beans or French beans
coarse salt	pickling salt
6 pints/3½ litres vinegar	15 cups (7½ pints) vinegar
2 teaspoons mustard seeds	2 teaspoons mustard seeds
12 chillis, crushed finely	12 chilis, crushed finely
2 oz./50 g. ground turmeric	½ cup ground turmeric
1½ oz./40 g. dry mustard	scant ⅓ cup dry mustard
8 oz./225 g. fine sugar	1 cup fine sugar
1 tablespoon cornflour	1 tablespoon cornstarch

Peel the marrow, remove seeds and pulp, and cut into slices, 2 inches/5 cm. long and about ½ inch/1¼ cm. thick. Peel cucumber and cut into small chunks. Remove leaves from cauliflower, and break into small sprigs; peel shallots, remove ends and strings from beans and if they are big cut them into strips, though it is best to use small ones that will not need cutting.

Place all these on a large dish in layers, with a handful of coarse salt between the layers and a good sprinkling on top, and leave overnight. Shake off the excess salt and put the vegetables in a large pan. Well cover with the vinegar – a little more or less may be needed. Add the mustard seeds, and the chillis. Boil all together for 15 minutes.

Mix turmeric (a spice sold by grocers, chemists or herbalists), mustard, sugar and cornflour to a smooth paste with a little cold vinegar. Add this to the pickle after it has boiled for 15 minutes, let it return to the boil, and simmer for another 5–8 minutes – stirring all the time. Pour into hot jars, and tie down when cold.

Chow-Chow
Chinese piccalilli

Yield approx 6 lb./2¾ kg.

Imperial/Metric	American
1 lb./½ kg. cucumber, chopped (if gherkins are available, use tiny whole ones)	1 lb. cucumber, chopped (if dill pickles are available, use tiny whole ones)
1 lb./½ kg. green tomatoes, sliced	1 lb. green tomatoes, sliced
1 lb./½ kg. onions, sliced	1 lb. onions, sliced
1 lb./½ kg. small shallots	1 lb. small shallots
1 lb./½ kg. cauliflower, cut into flowerets	1 lb. cauliflower, cut into flowerets
1 lb./½ kg. celery, chopped	1 lb. celery, chopped
2 oz./50 g. coarse salt	3 tablespoons pickling salt
4 pints/2¼ litres cold water	10 cups (5 pints) cold water
2 oz./50 g. flour	½ cup flour
1½ tablespoons dry mustard	2 tablespoons dry mustard
½ teaspoon ground turmeric	½ teaspoon ground turmeric
8 oz. less 2 tablespoons/200 g. sugar	1 cup sugar
2 pints/generous litre spiced vinegar (see page 40)	5 cups spiced vinegar (see page 40)

Place prepared vegetables in large pan. Cover with brine made from the salt and water. Stand for 24 hours, covered. Heat slowly to boiling point and then drain, and keep hot.

Mix flour, mustard, turmeric and sugar until well blended. Mix to a smooth paste with a little of the vinegar. Heat rest of vinegar in top of a double boiler. Do not boil. When hot, slowly add the vinegar paste and cook until thick, still not allowing mixture to boil.

Add to hot vegetables. Cook 10–15 minutes. Pack into clean hot jars and seal.

Mustard Sweet Pickle

Yield approx 9 lb./4 kg.

Imperial/Metric	American
1 medium marrow	1 medium summer squash
1 cauliflower	1 cauliflower
1 cucumber	1 cucumber
1 lb./½ kg. onions	1 lb. onions
1 lb./½ kg. young French beans	1 lb. young French or green beans
1 oz./25 g. coarse salt	1½ tablespoons pickling salt
2 oz./50 g. dry mustard	½ cup dry mustard
½ oz./15 g. ground turmeric	2½ tablespoons ground turmeric
¼ oz./8 g. ground ginger	scant 2 tablespoons ground ginger
½ oz./15 g. ground nutmeg	2½ tablespoons ground nutmeg
10 oz./300 g. sugar	1⅓ cups sugar
2 oz./50 g. flour	½ cup flour
2 pints/generous litre vinegar	5 cups vinegar

Chop the vegetables into ½-inch/1¼-cm.–1-inch/2½-cm. chunks. Sprinkle with the salt, cover with water and soak overnight, then drain off the water. Mix all dry ingredients with a little of the vinegar to make a smooth paste. Add remainder of the vinegar to the vegetables and simmer in a strong pan until barely tender, approximately 10 minutes. Add some boiling vinegar to the blended ingredients, then add them to the pan, boil for 10 minutes, stirring all the time and allow to thicken. Pot while hot.

Apple and Cucumber Pickle

Yield approx 3 2-pint/1¼ litre/5-cup jars

Imperial/Metric	American
3 lb./1½ kg. red-skinned apples, cored and sliced	3 lb. red-skinned apples, cored and sliced
2 large cucumbers, sliced	2 large cucumbers, sliced
2 pints/generous litre water	5 cups water
juice of 3 lemons	juice of 3 lemons
4 tablespoons salt	5 tablespoons salt
1 lb./½ kg. brown sugar	1 lb. brown sugar
1½ pints/9 dl. cider	3¾ cups cider
1½ pints/9 dl. vinegar	3¾ cups vinegar

Place prepared apple and cucumber in a large bowl. Cover with a lemon brine (made by mixing the water, lemon juice and salt) and leave to stand for 4 hours. Drain and rinse in fresh cold water. Bring sugar, cider and vinegar to boiling point. Add drained apple and cucumber and simmer for 3 minutes. Pack cucumber and apple into sterilised jars, and pour liquid over until overflowing. Seal.

Shown in colour on page 55

Pickled Mushrooms

Yield approx 1½ lb./¾ kg.

Imperial/Metric	American
1 lb./½ kg. button mushrooms	1 lb. button mushrooms
about 1 pint/6 dl. white vinegar	about 2½ cups white vinegar
1 teaspoon coarse salt	1 teaspoon pickling salt
½ teaspoon white pepper	½ teaspoon white pepper
small piece root ginger	small piece root ginger
1 small onion, sliced	1 small onion, sliced

Clean mushrooms by wiping them over with a damp flannel dipped in salt; it is not necessary to peel them. Put into pan with white vinegar to cover them, and add rest of ingredients. Simmer until mushrooms are tender, lift them out carefully and place in jar, then cover with hot vinegar. Seal well.

Corn Pickle

Yield approx 3 lb./1½ kg.

Imperial/Metric	American
1 cucumber, peeled	1 cucumber, peeled
3 onions, peeled	3 onions, peeled
1 green pepper, seeded	1 green sweet pepper, seeded
4 tomatoes, peeled and seeded	4 tomatoes, peeled and seeded
2½ lb./1¼ kg. corn kernels (approx. 5 cobs) or 3 (12-oz./350-g.) cans kernel corn	2½ lb. corn kernels (approx. 5 cobs) or 3 (12-oz.) cans kernel corn
8 oz./225 g. sugar	1 cup sugar
2 level tablespoons coarse salt	2–3 tablespoons pickling salt
½ teaspoon black pepper	½ teaspoon black pepper
½ pint/3 dl. cider vinegar	1¼ cups cider vinegar
¼ pint/1½ dl. water	⅔ cup water
½ teaspoon ground turmeric	½ teaspoon ground turmeric
1½ teaspoons dry mustard	1½ teaspoons dry mustard

Cut the cucumber and onion into ½-inch/1¼-cm. dice. Cut the pepper and tomatoes similarly. Put all the ingredients except the tomatoes into a large saucepan. Bring to the boil, stirring. Boil for 5 minutes until the sugar has dissolved. Cover and simmer gently for 1 hour. Add the tomatoes and cook for a further 5 minutes. Pour into warm, sterilised preserving jars and screw tops tightly. If jam jars are used, cover the pickle with waxed paper and seal jars with cellophane and a rubber band. Keep for 4–5 weeks before use.

Tomato and Apple Pickle

Yield approx 7–8 lb./3½ kg.

Imperial/Metric	American
6 lb./3 kg. tomatoes	6 lb. tomatoes
1 lb./½ kg. apples	1 lb. apples
2 onions	2 onions
1 oz./25 g. mustard seeds	2½ tablespoons mustard seeds
1 oz./25 g. ground ginger	4 tablespoons ground ginger
3 oz./75 g. coarse salt	¼ cup pickling salt
6 peppercorns	6 peppercorns
1½–2 pints/9 dl.–1¼ litres vinegar	3¾–5 cups vinegar
1 lb./½ kg. brown sugar	1 lb. brown sugar

Skin and cut up tomatoes, then put them in a large enamel pan; peel and core apples and cut them into rough pieces. Peel and chop onions finely and add to the tomatoes and apples in the pan, together with spices, salt, peppercorns and vinegar. Bring to the boil and simmer until the apples begin to soften, then add the sugar. Stir until sugar dissolves, and continue simmering until all is reduced to a pulp. Stir well, and leave to cool. Pour pickle into jars, and cover when it is quite cold.

Corn Relish

Yield approx 5 lb./2¼ kg.

Imperial/Metric	American
2¼ lb./1 kg. corn kernels, fresh or canned	2¼ lb. (6½ cups) kernel corn, fresh or canned
14 oz./400 g. white cabbage, chopped	4 cups white cabbage, chopped
5 oz./150 g. celery, finely chopped	1¼ cups celery, finely chopped
2 large red peppers, seeded	2 large red sweet peppers, seeded
2 large green peppers, seeded	2 large green sweet peppers, seeded
1 medium onion	1 medium onion
2 lb./1 kg. sugar	2 lb. sugar
1 tablespoon coarse salt	1 tablespoon pickling salt
1 tablespoon dry mustard	1 tablespoon dry mustard
1½ pints/9 dl. white or cider vinegar	3¾ cups white or cider vinegar

Mince or chop the vegetables. Mix with rest of ingredients, cook until corn is tender – about 15 minutes. Bottle and seal. If canned corn is used, cooking time can be cut to 8–10 minutes.

Corn relish; making mustard pickle

Peppered Apple Rings

Yield 3–4 1-lb./½-kg. jars

Imperial/Metric	American
4 lb./2 kg. dessert apples, peeled, cored and cut into rings	4 lb. dessert apples, pared, cored and cut into rings
2 lb./1 kg. green peppers, seeded and cut into rings	2 lb. green sweet peppers, seeded and cut into rings
3 pints/1½ litres cider vinegar	7½ cups cider vinegar
4 oz./125 g. brown sugar	½ cup brown sugar, firmly packed
2 tablespoons juniper berries	2–3 tablespoons juniper berries

Pack apple and pepper rings into hot sterilised jars in layers. Bring the vinegar, sugar and juniper berries to the boil, and immediately pour over the apple and pepper rings, allowing it to overflow the jars. Seal at once.

The flavour improves if the jars are left for 6 weeks or more before opening – the vinegar syrup then has time to penetrate fully the apple and peppers.

Peppered apple rings

Spiced Cherries

Imperial/Metric	American
2 lb./1 kg. red or Morello cherries	2 lb. red or Morello cherries
1 pint/6 dl. white vinegar, spiced (see page 40)	2½ cups white vinegar, spiced (see page 40)
1 lb./½ kg. Demerara sugar	1 lb. raw sugar

The fruit should be perfect and just ripe. Wash it and if red eating cherries are used remove stalks; if Morello cherries are used cut off the stalks, leaving ½-inch/1-cm. length attached to fruit. Heat the vinegar and sugar gently until sugar is dissolved, then add cherries and simmer about 5 minutes until cherries are tender but unbroken. Take out cherries with draining spoon and put into sterilised jars. Boil vinegar and sugar until syrupy, cool slightly, then pour over the cherries. Leave overnight then strain the syrup back into saucepan and reboil it, cool, and pour back over cherries. Leave to go quite cold. Cover with plastic lids, or glass covers and screw-bands. Metal should never come into contact with syrup or fruit.

In all cases, the spiced fruit should be completely covered with syrup. After the first filling of the jars, when they are left to soak overnight, some syrup may be lost through the fruit absorbing it; in this case a little extra vinegar and sugar should be added in the second boiling of the syrup.

Sweet Spiced Apple Pieces

Yield approx 3–4 2-pint/1-litre/5-cup jars

Imperial/Metric	American
4 lb./2 kg. preserving or granulated sugar	4 lb. sugar
2 pints/1¼ litres water	5 cups water
¼ pint/1½ dl. ginger wine	⅔ cup ginger wine
1-inch/2½-cm. stick of cinnamon	1-inch stick of cinnamon
1 blade mace	1 piece mace
small piece ginger root	small piece ginger root
5–6 cloves	5–6 cloves
4 lb./2 kg. apples, cored and cut into eighths	4 lb. apples, cored and cut into eighths
thinly pared rind of 2 lemons	thinly pared rind of 2 lemons

Boil sugar and water and ginger wine with the cinnamon stick, a piece of mace, ginger root, and the cloves, for 10 minutes. Strain liquid into a clean pan. Add the apple pieces and lemon rind, cook until tender and syrup thick. Add fresh samples of all the spices and pour into sterilised jars; seal. (The syrup may be tinted with colouring if wished.)

Shown in colour on page 55

Pickled Plums

Yield approx 2 lb./1 kg.

Imperial/Metric	American
2 lb./1 kg. cooking plums	2 lb. cooking plums
rind of ½ lemon	rind of ½ lemon
1 tablespoon allspice berries	1 tablespoon allspice berries
1 piece root ginger	1 piece root ginger
2 teaspoons whole cloves	2 teaspoons whole cloves
3-inch/7½-cm. stick of cinnamon	3-inch stick of cinnamon
½ tablespoon coriander seeds	½ tablespoon coriander seeds
1 pint/6 dl. vinegar	2½ cups vinegar
8 oz./225 g. brown sugar	1 cup brown sugar

Wash and stalk plums. Put in a large enamel pan, add the lemon rind, and the spices tied in a piece of muslin. Pour in the vinegar. Cover, and bring to simmering point slowly; the plums should never boil. Remove plums with a draining spoon, and pack into clean hot jars. Reheat the vinegar and spices, add the sugar, and boil until mixture becomes syrupy. Remove bag of spices. Fill jars with the liquid, making sure that all the plums are completely covered. Seal at once with synthetic skin, or air-tight closures, but make sure that no metal comes into contact with the plums. Store in a dark cool cupboard for at least 2 months; serve with cold meat, or with cheese.

Spiced Plums

Imperial/Metric	American
1½ lb./¾ kg. Victoria plums	1½ lb. dessert plums
¾ pint/4½ dl. white vinegar	scant 2 cups white vinegar
1½ lb./700 g. granulated sugar	1½ lb. granulated sugar
1½ oz./40 g. stick of cinnamon	1½ oz. stick of cinnamon
½ oz./15 g. whole allspice	½ oz. whole allspice
½ oz./15 g. mixed spice	2 tablespoons mixed spices

Wipe the plums with a cloth wrung out in hot water. Remove stalks. Discard any bruised plums. Boil vinegar, sugar and spices together until syrupy. Arrange the plums upright in sterilised, wide-necked jars. Allow the syrup to cool, then pour over the plums. Leave until next day, then strain off syrup, reboil it, cool and pour over plums. When quite cold cover jars with plastic-lined lids and screw-caps. Store in cool, dark place. Keep 3 to 4 months before using.

Spiced Grapes

Imperial/Metric	American
2 lb./1 kg. firm, but ripe grapes (the small seedless kind are best)	2 lb. firm, but ripe grapes (the small seedless kind are best)
½ pint/3 dl. white vinegar	1¼ cups white vinegar
1 lb./½ kg. granulated sugar	1 lb. granulated sugar
4-inch/10-cm. stick of cinnamon	4-inch stick of cinnamon
12 cloves	12 cloves
½ nutmeg, grated	½ nutmeg, grated

Wash the grapes and break them into small bunches. Put vinegar in a pan, put in the sugar, heat gently until dissolved, then bring to the boil. Add the grapes and the spices and simmer gently for 5 minutes. Put the bunches of grapes into jars and pour the spiced liquid over them to cover. Leave until the next day, then strain off the liquid into saucepan. Bring to the boil. Remove the cinnamon from the grapes. Allow the liquid to cool, then fill up the jars again, to cover the fruit. Tie down, using waxed paper or polythene.

Spiced Orange Slices

Yield approx 2 lb./1 kg.

Imperial/Metric	American
4 thin-skinned oranges	4 thin-skinned oranges
water	water
pinch bicarbonate of soda	pinch baking soda
½ pint/3 dl. white vinegar	1¼ cups white vinegar
16 cloves	16 cloves
4 blades mace	4 pieces mace
4-inch/10-cm. stick of cinnamon	4-inch stick of cinnamon
4 bay leaves	4 bay leaves
12 oz./350 g. granulated sugar	1½ cups sugar, firmly packed

Wipe the oranges and put them in a pan with cold water to cover adding bicarbonate of soda. Bring to the boil and simmer for 30–40 minutes, until the skin can easily be pierced with a knitting needle. Drain off the water, but reserve it. Allow oranges to cool, then cut them in slices across, about ¼ inch/½ cm. thick, and cut the slices in halves. Put vinegar, ½ pint (3 dl., 1¼ cups) orange liquid and sugar into a pan. Tie cloves, mace, cinnamon and bay leaves in muslin and add to liquid. Bring to the boil, simmer for 20 minutes, then put in the orange slices (discarding any pips) and simmer gently for 30 minutes. Put oranges and spiced liquid in a bowl and leave overnight.

Next day, take out the bag of spices and put orange slices into jars. Boil up the spiced liquid again, leave to cool slightly, then pour over the oranges. When cold, tie down, using waxed paper or sheet polythene to cover.

Spiced Peaches or Pears

Yield approx 3 1-lb./½-kg. jars

Imperial/Metric	American
2 lb./1 kg. firm peaches	2 lb. firm peaches
½ pint/3 dl. white wine vinegar	1¼ cups white wine vinegar
1 lb./½ kg. granulated sugar	1 lb. sugar
½ oz./15 g. cloves	½ oz. cloves
6-inch/15-cm. stick of cinnamon	6-inch stick of cinnamon
¼ oz./8 g. whole allspice	¼ oz. whole allspice
6 extra cloves	6 extra cloves
3 extra small pieces cinnamon	3 extra small pieces cinnamon

Dip the peaches in boiling water and remove skins by gently pressing them with the thumbs. Small or medium peaches can be pickled whole, but large ones should be halved. Bring the vinegar, sugar and spices to the boil, then add the peaches and simmer until tender. Remove them with a perforated spoon to drain the liquid, and pack into heated jars. Boil the vinegar and spices again until syrupy, then strain into jars. Add 2 cloves and a piece of cinnamon to each jar. Cover and screw down immediately.

Keep at least a week before using.

Pears

Pears may be spiced and pickled in the same way. As each pear is peeled put it at once into the boiling spiced vinegar, as pears discolour after peeling.

Pears in Heavy Syrup

Yield approx 4–5 lb./2 kg.

Imperial/Metric	American
3 lb./1½ kg. granulated or loaf sugar	3 lb. sugar, granulated or cube
1 pint/6 dl. water	2½ cups water
rind and juice of 3 lemons	rind and juice of 3 lemons
1-inch/2½-cm. piece root ginger	1-inch piece root ginger
4 lb./2 kg. firm-ripe pears	4 lb. firm-ripe pears

Put the sugar, water, lemon rind and juice, and ginger in an enamel pan and bring to the boil. Peel the pears, keeping on the stalks; if large, pears may be halved, but they are less likely to break if kept whole. As each pear is prepared, put it straight into the boiling liquid. When all pears are in, cover pan closely and simmer very gently until quite tender, but not broken. Take them up carefully with perforated spoon and place in hot jars. Keep the liquid in the pan boiling all the time you are doing this.

As each jar is filled with pears, strain the syrup over them and cover and screw down immediately. Try to arrange the pears upright in the jars, without

overcrowding them; they are less likely to crush and lose their shape this way.

Ready for use within a few days.

Pear and Orange Slices in Liqueur

Yield approx 3 2-pint/1¼-litre jars

Imperial/Metric	American
4 lb./2 kg. preserving or granulated sugar	4 lb. preserving or granulated sugar
2 pints/1¼ litres water	5 cups water
12 cloves	12 cloves
4 lb./2 kg. dessert pears, peeled, cored and quartered	4 lb. dessert pears, pared, cored and quartered
6 thin-skinned oranges, thinly sliced and pipped	6 thin-skinned oranges, thinly sliced and seeded
1 miniature bottle of Grand Marnier	1 miniature bottle of Grand Marnier

Boil sugar, water and cloves for 10 minutes. Add pears and orange slices. Cook until pears are clear and the syrup thick. Allow fruit to stand in syrup for 3 hours, after cooking – this results in plump preserves. Add liqueur, reheat just to boiling point, pour into jars, removing cloves, and seal at once.

Marrow and Apple Chutney

Yield approx 6½–7 lb./3 kg.

Imperial/Metric	American
3 lb./1½ kg. marrow, after peeling and seeding	3 lb. summer squash, after paring and seeding
1½ lb./¾ kg. onions	1½ lb. onions
2 tablespoons coarse salt	3 tablespoons pickling salt
2 lb./1 kg. apples, after peeling and coring	2 lb. apples, after paring and coring
1½ lb./¾ kg. brown sugar	1½ lb. brown sugar
3 pints/1½ litres spiced vinegar (see page 40)	7½ cups spiced vinegar (see page 40)

Cut the marrow into slices, peel and chop onions. Put marrow and onions in shallow dish, sprinkling with coarse salt; leave 24 hours, then strain. Slice apples, put in a pan with marrow and onions and sugar. Cook in half the vinegar until tender and apples are pulpy, stirring from time to time. Add remaining vinegar and simmer until reduced and thickened. Pot up while still hot and cover at once.

Ready to eat immediately.

Windfall cooking apples can be used for chutney making, as long as all bruised parts are removed. Be sure to get the correct weight of sound fruit.

Working mixture through Mouli grater

Ladling purée into pots

Apple and Tomato Chutney

Yield approx 6–7 1-lb./½-kg. jars

Imperial/Metric	American
3 lb./1½ kg. tomatoes	3 lb. tomatoes
3 lb./1½ kg. cooking apples, cored	3 lb. cooking apples, cored
1 lb./½ kg. onions, peeled	1 lb. onions, peeled
1 green pepper (optional)	1 green sweet pepper (optional)
8 oz./225 g. sultanas	½ lb. seedless white raisins
8 oz./225 g. Demerara sugar	1 cup raw sugar
½ oz./15 g. salt	scant 1 tablespoon salt
¼ oz./8 g. bruised root ginger	¼ oz. bruised root ginger
½ oz./15 g. red chillis	½ oz. red chilis
2 teaspoons pickling spice	2 teaspoons pickling spice
2 pints/generous litre vinegar	5 cups vinegar

Mince together the tomatoes, apples, onions, pepper and sultanas, place in a pan with the sugar, salt and spices tied in muslin, stir in the vinegar, bring to the boil and boil gently without a lid until reduced to a thick consistency. This will take about 1 hour. Remove the spice bag, put mixture through Mouli grater (see above), pot and cover.

Spicy Apple Chutney

Yield approx 5 lb./2¼ kg.

Imperial/Metric	American
1 lb./½ kg. onions, peeled and minced or finely chopped	1 lb. onions, peeled and ground or finely chopped
5 lb./2¼ kg. apples, peeled and minced or finely chopped	5 lb. apples, pared and ground or finely chopped
½ pint/3 dl. water	1¼ cups water
1 teaspoon ground ginger	1 teaspoon ground ginger
2 teaspoons salt	2 teaspoons salt
4 teaspoons dry mustard	4 teaspoons dry mustard
12 cloves and 6 allspice, tied in muslin bag	12 cloves and 6 allspice, tied in cheesecloth bag
¾ pint/4½ dl. vinegar	scant 2 cups vinegar
1 lb./½ kg. brown sugar	1 lb. brown sugar

Put the onions, apples, water, ginger, salt and mustard into a large saucepan. Add bag of spice. Stir well, bring to the boil then simmer gently for 45 minutes.

Add vinegar and sugar and simmer, uncovered, for 1½–2 hours, or until chutney takes on a jam-like consistency. Remove muslin bag, cool, bottle and cover.

Apple and Mint Chutney

Yield approx 4 lb./1¾ kg.

Imperial/Metric	American
2 lb./1 kg. apples	2 lb. apples
1 pint/6 dl. mint leaves	2½ cups mint leaves
8 oz./225 g. onions	½ lb. onions
8 oz./225 g. tomatoes	½ lb. tomatoes
1 lb./450 g. currants	1 lb. currants
1 pint/6 dl. vinegar	2½ cups vinegar
2 teaspoons dry mustard	2 teaspoons dry mustard
2 teaspoons salt	2 teaspoons salt
12 oz./350 g. brown sugar	1½ cups brown sugar, firmly packed

Peel, core and mince apples finely with mint leaves, onions, tomatoes and currants. Add ¾ pint (4½ dl., 2 cups) vinegar, mustard and salt, and cook until soft. Pour ¼ pint (1½ dl., ⅔ cup) heated vinegar over the sugar and stir to dissolve. Add to the cooked ingredients and simmer again until thick.

Norwich apple chutney

Norwich Apple Chutney

Yield approx 4 lb./1¾ kg.

Imperial/Metric	American
2½ lb./1¼ kg. apples, peeled and cored	2½ lb. apples, pared and cored
8 oz./225 g. onions, peeled	½ lb. onions, peeled
¾ pint/4½ dl. spiced vinegar (see page 40)	2 cups spiced vinegar (see page 40)
8 oz./225 g. brown sugar	1 cup brown sugar, firmly packed
4 oz./125 g. sultanas	¾ cup seedless white raisins
½ oz./15 g. salt	good 2 teaspoons salt
½ tablespoon dry mustard	½ tablespoon dry mustard
1 teaspoon coriander seeds (optional)	1 teaspoon coriander seeds (optional)
2 pieces root ginger	2 pieces root ginger

Mince or finely chop the apples and onions. Simmer with half quantity of vinegar until tender. Add sugar, sultanas, salt, mustard, coriander seeds, ginger and remainder of vinegar. Simmer until thick, about 20 minutes. Remove ginger and turn into heated jars while hot; firmly place on glass lids.

If ordinary jars are used, a cover should be used to stop the vinegar evaporating, for example, good corks or a layer of thick, vinegar-proof waxed paper, then a plastic or cork-lined metal lid and screwbands.

Apple Mint Jelly

Imperial/Metric	American
4 lb./1¾ kg. Bramley cooking apples	4 lb. cooking apples
1½ pints/9 dl. water	3¾ cups water
6 sprigs mint	6 sprigs mint
sugar	sugar
¾ pint/4½ dl. measure chopped mint	scant 2 cups chopped mint
¾ pint/4½ dl. white vinegar	scant 2 cups white vinegar
few drops green vegetable colouring	few drops green vegetable coloring

Wash apples, cut them up roughly (do not peel or core them) and cook them in the water, adding the 6 sprigs of mint, until reduced to a pulp, stirring often. Pour pulp into a jelly bag or two thicknesses of muslin and leave to drip overnight into a basin (see page 15). Next day measure the juice, put into a clean pan, and allow 1 lb./½ kg. sugar to each 1 pint (6 dl., 2½ cups) of juice. Add the vinegar, stir over a low heat until sugar is dissolved then bring quickly to the boil. Add the chopped mint, and boil steadily until a good set is reached when a little is tested on a cold plate (see page 8).

When setting point is reached, add a few drops green colouring, continue to boil for a minute then stir well, and remove from heat. Allow to stand until a fine skin forms on top, then stir well to disperse the mint evenly. Pour into small pots, and tie down when cold.
This is an excellent substitute for mint sauce in winter. Rhubarb or gooseberry juice can be used instead of apple juice.

Apple and red pepper chutney. Pear and apricot, Apple and apricot, Apple and fig jams, Apple and cinnamon butter, see recipes, pages 11, 12, 13, 14. Mint sauce, see recipe, page 58

Apple and Red Pepper Chutney

Yield approx 6–7 1-lb./½-kg. jars

Imperial/Metric	American
4 lb./1¾ kg. apples	4 lb. apples
1 lb./½ kg. red peppers	1 lb. red sweet peppers
1½ lb./¾ kg. onions	1½ lb. onions
8 oz./225 g. raisins	1½ cups raisins
4 oz./125 g. sultanas	¾ cup seedless white raisins
4 oz./125 g. currants	¾ cup currants
1 lb./½ kg. brown sugar plus 1	1 lb. brown sugar plus 1
tablespoon	tablespoon
1 tablespoon black treacle	1 tablespoon dark molasses
1 pint/6 dl. vinegar	2½ cups vinegar
1 tablespoon salt	1 tablespoon salt
pinch of cayenne pepper	pinch of cayenne
a few spices as used in making	a few spices as used in making
spiced vinegar	spiced vinegar

Peel, core and chop the apples finely, seed and chop peppers, slice the onions, stone and chop raisins and sultanas, clean the currants. Put all in pan with sugar and treacle, vinegar, salt and pinch of cayenne. Simmer gently for 1 hour, stirring frequently. Put into jars with a few spices in each jar and tie down securely.

Raspberry jam, Pear and marrow ginger, see recipes, pages 9, 12

Gooseberry Chutney

Yield approx $3\frac{1}{2}$–4 lb./$1\frac{3}{4}$–2 kg.

Imperial/Metric	American
8 oz./225 g. onions	$\frac{1}{2}$ lb. onions
3 lb./$1\frac{1}{2}$ kg. green gooseberries	3 lb. green gooseberries
12 oz./350 g. soft brown sugar	$1\frac{1}{2}$ cups soft brown (Barbados) sugar, firmly packed
$1\frac{1}{2}$ pints/9 dl. spiced vinegar (see page 40)	$3\frac{3}{4}$ pints spiced vinegar (see page 40)
$\frac{1}{2}$ oz./15 g. mustard seeds	4 teaspoons mustard seeds
1 oz./25 g. salt	$1\frac{1}{2}$ tablespoons salt
6 oz./175 g. seedless raisins	1 cup seedless raisins

Peel and roughly chop onions. Top and tail gooseberries, wash well. Place gooseberries and onions in preserving pan, add remaining ingredients, stir well. Simmer in uncovered pan for about 1 hour, until smooth and thick. Pour chutney into clean hot jars and cover and tie down firmly. When cold, keep in cool dark place.

Dried Fruit Chutney

Yield approx 7–8 lb./$3\frac{1}{2}$ kg.

Imperial/Metric	American
1 lb./$\frac{1}{2}$ kg. seedless raisins	3 cups seedless raisins
8 oz./225 g. cooking dates, chopped small	$1\frac{1}{2}$ cups cooking dates, chopped small
8 oz./225 g. currants	$1\frac{1}{2}$ cups currants
8 oz./225 g. dried apricots, soaked overnight and chopped	$1\frac{1}{2}$ cups dried apricots, soaked overnight and chopped
2 lb./1 kg. apples, after peeling, coring and slicing	2 lb. apples, after paring, coring and slicing
3 large onions, chopped	3 large onions, chopped
3 pints/$1\frac{1}{2}$ litres vinegar	$7\frac{1}{2}$ cups vinegar
1 oz./25 g. chillis, crushed	1 oz. chilis, crushed
2 oz./50 g. bruised root ginger	2 oz. bruised root ginger
1 lb./450 g. soft brown sugar	1 lb. soft brown sugar

Put all the fruit and onions in pan with the vinegar; add chillis and ginger wrapped in muslin. Simmer until the apples are mushy, stirring often. Remove the chillis and ginger. Add the sugar; boil for a further 10 minutes, until chutney thickens. Stir often to prevent sticking. Pour into hot jars; tie down when cold.

This is a mild 'all-year-round' chutney. In the North of England it is often spread on bread and butter, like jam. For a hotter chutney use spiced vinegar.

Apple and prune chutney; Pear, date and nut chutney, see recipe, page 54

Apple and Prune Chutney

Yield approx $4\frac{1}{2}$ lb./2 kg.

Imperial/Metric	American
4 lb./$1\frac{3}{4}$ kg. cooking apples, peeled, cored and chopped	4 lb. cooking apples, pared, cored and chopped
1 lb./$\frac{1}{2}$ kg. prunes, soaked and stoned	1 lb. prunes, soaked and pitted
$\frac{3}{4}$ pint/$4\frac{1}{2}$ dl. vinegar	2 cups vinegar
juice of 4 lemons	juice of 4 lemons
12 oz./350 g. sugar	$1\frac{1}{2}$ cups sugar, firmly packed
2 teaspoons salt	2 teaspoons salt

Place all ingredients in a large saucepan and simmer together for 1 hour, or until quite thick. Pour into hot sterilised jars and seal immediately.

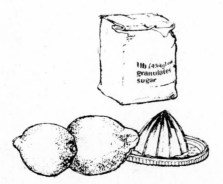

Australian sweet chutney

Australian Sweet Chutney
using Australian dried fruits

Yield approx 9 lb./4 kg.

Imperial/Metric	American
3 lb./1½ kg. Granny Smith apples	3 lb. hard green apples
1 lb./450 g. stoned raisins	1 lb. seeded raisins
8 oz./¼ kg. onions	½ lb. onions
1 lb./½ kg. tomatoes	1 lb. tomatoes
2½ lb./1¼ kg. brown sugar	2½ lb. brown sugar
4 oz./125 g. currants	1 cup currants
1 teaspoon ground cloves	1 teaspoon ground cloves
1 oz./25 g. chopped, preserved ginger	1 oz. chopped, preserved (Canton) ginger
½ tablespoon dry mustard	½ tablespoon dry mustard
¼ teaspoon cayenne pepper	¼ teaspoon cayenne pepper
1 tablespoon salt	1 tablespoon salt
1½ pints/9 dl. vinegar	3¾ cups vinegar

Peel and core apples and stew them gently in a very small quantity of water until tender. Chop raisins and onions and skin tomatoes. Place all ingredients in a saucepan and simmer gently for 1½ hours. Place in sterilised jars and cover.

Orange Chutney

Yield approx 1½–2 lb./¾–1 kg.

Imperial/Metric	American
3 navel oranges	3 navel oranges
2 medium apples	2 medium apples
1 large onion	1 large onion
8 oz./225 g. brown sugar	1 cup brown sugar, firmly packed
4 oz./125 g. raisins	¾ cup seedless raisins
2 oz./50 g. ground ginger	½ cup ground ginger
¼ oz./8 g. chillis, crushed	¼ oz. chilis, crushed
1 pint/6 dl. malt vinegar	2½ cups malt vinegar
1 oz./25 g. salt	1½ tablespoons salt
pinch of black pepper	pinch of black pepper

Grate yellow orange skins, remove pith, skin and pips, cut oranges into small pieces. Peel the apples and chop finely, removing core and pips. Peel and chop onion. Put all into an enamel pan with the sugar, cleaned raisins, ginger, chillis, vinegar, salt and pepper. Bring to the boil, stirring well, then simmer gently until the fruit is tender and reduced to a pulp – about 40 minutes. Stir often to prevent sticking. Pour off into hot jars and cover immediately.

The large South African navel oranges are best for this chutney as they are very juicy and have few pips. This is a 'sweet and hot' pickle, but you can use less ginger if you like a milder flavour.

Orange and Apricot Chutney

Yield approx 9–10 lb./4½–5 kg.

Imperial/Metric	American
4 oranges	4 oranges
2 lb./1 kg. dried apricots, chopped and soaked overnight	2 lb. dried apricots, chopped and soaked overnight
2 large onions, chopped	2 large onions, chopped
1½ lb./¾ kg. Demerara sugar	1½ lb. raw sugar
2 teaspoons coriander seeds, crushed	2 teaspoons coriander seeds, crushed
1 tablespoon salt	1 tablespoon salt
4 oz./125 g. sultanas	¾ cup seedless white raisins
1 pint/6 dl. white vinegar	2½ cups white vinegar

Boil oranges for 5 minutes. Cool, then pare thinly with a potato peeler. Cut peel into thin strips. Chop the pulp, over a bowl to collect all the juice, remove pith. Strain apricots, put them in pan with rest of ingredients, mix well, then add vinegar. Simmer gently for about 1–1¼ hours or until apricots are soft and chutney is thick, stir often. Pot at once into clean, hot jars, cover and keep in dry, dark place.

Sweet Pickle or Chutney

Yield approx 7–8 lb./3½ kg.

Imperial/Metric	American
4 lb./1¾ kg. green apples or 1 lb./ ½ kg. dried apple rings soaked in ¾ pint/4½ dl. water	4 lb. green apples or 1 lb. dried apple rings soaked in scant 2 cups water
1 lb./½ kg. tomatoes, green, red or mixed	1 lb. tomatoes, green, red or mixed
1 lb./450 g. currants	1 lb. currants
1 lb./450 g. sultanas	1 lb. seedless white raisins
1 lb./½ kg. onions, chopped	4 cups chopped onions
1 lb./½ kg. melon or marrow, chopped	3 cups chopped melon or summer squash
8 oz./225 g. gooseberries	½ lb. gooseberries
12 oz./350 g. brown sugar	1½ cups brown sugar, firmly packed
2 oz./50 g. ground ginger	½ cup ground ginger
1 oz./25 g. mustard seeds	2½ tablespoons mustard seeds
1 oz./25 g. salt	2 tablespoons salt
4–5 pints/2½–3 litres vinegar	10–12½ cups (5–6½ pints) vinegar

Peel and core apples and cut into slices; skin tomatoes and cut up roughly. Put in a large pan with other ingredients and cover with vinegar. Bring to the boil and simmer 45 minutes–1 hour, stirring frequently. Apples should be pulpy and sultanas soft. Pour into heated jars and tie down.

Add extra vinegar if the chutney evaporates too much before apples are cooked.

Indian Chutney

Yield approx 4–5 lb./2 kg.

Imperial/Metric	American
1 lb./½ kg. apples	1 lb. apples
1 lb./½ kg. onions	1 lb. onions
1 lb./½ kg. dates	1 lb. dates
1 teaspoon cayenne pepper	1 teaspoon cayenne
1 teaspoon ground ginger	1 teaspoon ground ginger
1 teaspoon dry mustard	1 teaspoon dry mustard
2 pints/generous litre spiced vinegar (see page 40)	5 cups spiced vinegar (see page 40)
1 lb./½ kg. brown sugar	1 lb. brown sugar

Mince apples, onions and dates. Mix cayenne, ginger and mustard to a paste with a tablespoon of the vinegar. Bring apples, dates and onions to the boil in the vinegar, and simmer until soft. Add sugar and cayenne mixture, and boil for 3 minutes, stirring well. Pot into hot jars; tie down at once.

This chutney can be made at any time of the year, and is a good standby. Use less cayenne, ginger and mustard for a milder chutney.

Lemon Chutney

Yield approx 5–6 lb./2½ kg.

Imperial/Metric	American
2 lb./1 kg. lemons	2 lb. lemons
1 lb./½ kg. onions, peeled	1 lb. onions, peeled
8 oz./225 g. seedless raisins, washed and dried	2 cups seedless raisins, cleaned
2 oz./50 g. salt	4 tablespoons salt
2–2½ pints/1–1¼ litres spiced vinegar (see page 40)	5–6¼ cups spiced vinegar (see page 40)
½ teaspoon ground ginger	½ teaspoon ground ginger
1¾ lb./800 g. white sugar	1¾ lb. white sugar

Squeeze juice from lemons, discarding pips. Mince rind, pith and pulp with onions and raisins, or chop with a knife. Put in bowl with lemon juice and salt. Add about 1½ pints (9 dl., 3¾ cups) of the vinegar or enough just to cover the mixture. Cover and leave overnight. Next day, turn mixture into pan, stir in ginger, cover and cook gently for about 1 hour till lemon pieces and onion are quite tender.

Mix sugar with ½ pint (3 dl., 1¼ cups) of remaining vinegar, and stir into pan. Boil fast for about 20 minutes till mixture thickens.

Put into hot jars and seal while hot.

Pear, Date and Nut Chutney

Yield approx 3½ lb./1¾ kg.

Imperial/Metric	American
3 lb./1½ kg. pears, peeled, cored and chopped	3 lb. pears, pared, cored and chopped
½ pint/3 dl. wine vinegar	1¼ cups wine vinegar
juice of 3 lemons	juice of 3 lemons
8 oz./225 g. brown sugar	1 cup brown sugar
4 oz./125 g. seeded raisins	1 cup seedless raisins
4 oz./125 g. dates, chopped	1 cup chopped dates
8 oz./225 g. walnut halves	2 cups walnut halves
2 teaspoons salt	2 teaspoons salt

Place all ingredients in a large saucepan and simmer together for 1 hour, or until quite thick. Pour into hot sterilised jars and seal immediately.

Pickled red cabbage, see recipe, page 41
Apple and cucumber pickle, Sweet spiced apple pieces, see recipes, pages 43, 46

Country Garden Chutney

Yield approx 11–12 lb./5½ kg.

Imperial/Metric	American
3 lb./1½ kg. green cooking apples	3 lb. green cooking apples
4 pints/2¼ litres vinegar	10 cups (5 pints) vinegar
1 lb./½ kg. brown sugar	1 lb. brown sugar
4 oz./125 g. coarse salt	¼ lb. (6 tablespoons) pickling salt
1 tablespoon ground nutmeg	1 tablespoon ground nutmeg
1 teaspoon ground cinnamon	1 teaspoon ground cinnamon
½ oz./15 g. mustard seeds	4 teaspoons mustard seeds
3 lb./1½ kg. ripe plums, stoned and quartered	3 lb. ripe plums, pitted and quartered
2 lb./1 kg. red tomatoes, skinned and quartered	2 lb. red tomatoes, peeled and quartered
1 lb./½ kg. onions, peeled and chopped	1 lb. onions, peeled and chopped
3 ridge cucumbers, washed and chopped (not peeled)	3 ridge (outdoor) cucumbers, washed and chopped (not peeled)
2 small pieces root ginger	2 small pieces root ginger
12 peppercorns	12 peppercorns
12 cloves	12 cloves
6 chillis	6 chilis

Peel and slice apples, removing cores and bruised parts. Boil vinegar with sugar, salt, nutmeg, cinnamon and the mustard seed, then add the prepared fruits and vegetables. Put ginger, peppercorns, cloves and chillis in a piece of muslin and tie it on the handle of the preserving pan so that it is suspended in the vinegar. Simmer gently until reduced to a pulp, about 1½ hours. Pour into hot jars and cover tightly.

Green Tomato Chutney

Yield approx 6–7 lb./3 kg.

Imperial/Metric	American
5 lb./2¼ kg. green tomatoes	5 lb. green tomatoes
1 lb./½ kg. onions	1 lb. onions
1 oz./25 g. salt	2 tablespoons salt
1 lb./450 g. sugar	1 lb. sugar
2 pints/generous litre spiced vinegar (see page 40)	5 cups spiced vinegar (see page 40)
8 oz./225 g. raisins	1¼ cups seedless raisins
8 oz./225 g. sultanas	1¼ cups seedless white raisins
1 lb./½ kg. cooking apples, peeled, cored and sliced	1 lb. cooking apples, pared, cored and sliced

Slice the tomatoes and chop the onions, and mix in a basin with salt. Allow this to stand overnight.

Next day, add the sugar to the vinegar and bring to the boil; then add the raisins (which may be chopped), sultanas, and apples. Simmer for 10 minutes. Add the strained tomatoes and onions, and simmer until thick, about 1 hour. Pour into warmed jars while still hot.

Can be eaten straight away, but improves with keeping.

Ripe Tomato Chutney

Yield approx 3½–4 lb./1¾ kg.

Imperial/Metric	American
3 lb./1½ kg. ripe tomatoes	3 lb. ripe tomatoes
8 oz./¼ kg. onions	½ lb. onions
12 oz./350 g. cooking apples	¾ lb. cooking apples
8 oz./225 g. seedless raisins	2 cups seedless raisins
1 lb./450 g. brown sugar	1 lb. brown sugar
1 oz./25 g. coarse salt	2 tablespoons coarse salt
1½ pints/9 dl. spiced vinegar (see page 40)	3¾ cups spiced vinegar (see page 40)

Dip tomatoes in boiling water and skin them. Chop coarsely, removing stalk ends. Skin and chop onions; mix with chopped tomatoes.

Peel, core and chop apples. Put apples and raisins, sugar and salt in the vinegar and bring to the boil. Add tomatoes and onions and simmer 45 minutes–1 hour, or until thick, stirring often.

Put in heated jars and cover securely while hot.

Tomato Sauce

Yield approx 2 pints/generous litre/5 cups

Imperial/Metric	American
6 lb./2¾ kg. sound ripe tomatoes	6 lb. sound ripe tomatoes
8 oz./225 g. sugar	1 cup sugar
¼ oz./8 g. salt	good 1 teaspoon salt
pinch of cayenne pepper	pinch of cayenne
good pinch of paprika	good pinch of paprika
1 tablespoon tarragon vinegar	1 tablespoon tarragon vinegar
1½ pints/9 dl. spiced vinegar	3¾ cups spiced vinegar

Wipe and slice tomatoes; cook in uncovered pan until tender. Rub through a hair sieve. Return pulp to clean pan, heat, add sugar, salt, cayenne and paprika, stir until sugar is melted; boil gently, keeping stirred, until moderately thick. Add tarragon vinegar and spiced vinegar, continue boiling gently and stirring frequently until sauce is of thick cream consistency; in judging consistency, allow for sauce thickening up while cooling. While sauce is still hot, pour into hot bottles through a funnel, to reach 1 inch/2½ cm. from top; cork down at once with new corks previously brought to the boil in cold water and boiled for 15 minutes. When sauce is cold, cut corks level with top of bottles, cover with wax, or put on screw-tops.

Spiced tomato relish; Mustard sweet pickle, see recipe, page 43

Tomato Ketchup

Yield approx 1½–2 pints/1 litre/3¾–5 cups

Imperial/Metric	American
4 lb./1¾ kg. ripe tomatoes	4 lb. ripe tomatoes
2 shallots	2 shallots
1 clove of garlic	1 clove of garlic
2 bay leaves	2 bay leaves
½ teaspoon cayenne pepper	½ teaspoon cayenne
¼ teaspoon paprika	¼ teaspoon paprika
½ oz./15 g. salt	2 teaspoons salt
6 oz./175 g. sugar	¾ cup sugar
½ pint/3 dl. plus 1 tablespoon spiced vinegar (see page 40)	1¼ cups plus 1 tablespoon spiced vinegar (see page 40)
2 teaspoons cornflour	2 teaspoons cornstarch

Cut up tomatoes and put them in a pan with chopped shallots, garlic and bay leaves. Simmer until a pulp.

Remove the garlic and bay leaves, and rub through a sieve, pressing out as much pulp as possible. Return the pulp to a clean pan, add cayenne, paprika, salt and sugar and ½ pint (3 dl., 1¼ cups) vinegar, and simmer 15–20 minutes. Mix cornflour with remaining vinegar, add to the boiling purée. Pour into hot, sterilised, screw-top bottles, put in corks (first sterilised by boiling them for 20 minutes), and then the screwbands, fitted loosely.

Place in boiling water to come up to the tops of bottles and keep at this temperature 10 minutes. Take the bottles out of the water and screw down the metal bands securely.

Spiced Tomato Relish

Yield approx 5 lb./2¼ kg.

Imperial/Metric	American
1 lb./½ kg. tomatoes	1 lb. tomatoes
1 green pepper	1 green sweet pepper
1 lb./½ kg. onions	1 lb. onions
1 lb./½ kg. apples	1 lb. apples
3 cloves of garlic	3 cloves of garlic
½ pint/3 dl. vinegar	1¼ cups vinegar
12 oz./350 g. white sugar	1½ cups white sugar
1 tablespoon salt	1 tablespoon salt
1 tablespoon paprika	1 tablespoon paprika
1 teaspoon cayenne pepper	1 teaspoon cayenne
1 tablespoon mixed English mustard	1 tablespoon prepared English mustard
½ teaspoon mixed spice	½ teaspoon mixed spices
6-oz./175-g. can tomato purée	6-oz. can tomato paste

Dip tomatoes in boiling water for 1 minute, remove skins and cut up tomatoes. Remove pips from pepper and cut up with onions and apples. Chop garlic finely. Put these in pan with vinegar and simmer until tender and thick, about 30 minutes. Add other ingredients, boil for 3 minutes. Pot while hot.

Elderberry Ketchup

Yield approx 2 pints/1 litre/5 cups

Imperial/Metric	American
4 lb./1¾ kg. ripe elderberries	4 lb. ripe elderberries
2–2½ pints/1–1¼ litres vinegar	5–6¼ cups vinegar
1 teaspoon peppercorns	1 teaspoon peppercorns
½ teaspoon cloves	½ teaspoon cloves
1 teaspoon mace	1 teaspoon mace
shallots	shallots
1 tablespoon salt	1 tablespoon salt

Put the elderberries in a preserving pan and cover them with vinegar. Bring to the boil very slowly and simmer for 15 minutes, then strain off liquor while still hot. To this liquor, add peppercorns, cloves and mace, plus 4 shallots to every 1 pint (6 dl., 2½ cups) of liquor. Bring to the boil, add the salt and simmer for 10 minutes. Remove shallots.

While hot, pour ketchup into heated bottles, and seal with corks and screw-tops at once.

Blackberry Relish

Yield approx 2½–3 pints/1¼–1½ litres/6–7½ cups

Imperial/Metric	American
5–6 lb./2¼–2¾ kg. blackberries	5–6 lb. blackberries
1 teaspoon salt	1 teaspoon salt
1 oz./25 g. sugar	2 tablespoons sugar
1 teaspoon dry mustard	1 teaspoon dry mustard
½ teaspoon ground cloves	½ teaspoon ground cloves
½ teaspoon ground nutmeg	½ teaspoon ground nutmeg
½ teaspoon ground cinnamon	½ teaspoon ground cinnamon
1 pint/6 dl. vinegar	2½ cups vinegar

Make a purée by simmering the blackberries in just enough water to cover them. Strain through a fine sieve, pressing out as much pulp as possible. Put strained juice and pulp (about 2 pints/1 litre/5 cups) in an enamel saucepan and add the rest of the ingredients. Simmer for 10–15 minutes, then pour into heated bottles and seal down at once with corks and screwbands.

Sterilise in water bath (see page 28). Tighten screwbands immediately.

Thick Fruit Sauce

Yield approx 4–5 pints/2¼–3 litres/5–6½ pints

Imperial/Metric	American
7 lb./3¼ kg. firm red or green tomatoes (or a mixture of both)	7 lb. firm red or green tomatoes (or a mixture of both)
6 lb./2¾ kg. cooking apples	6 lb. cooking apples
2 lb./1 kg. onions	2 lb. onions
1 lb./½ kg. dates	1 lb. dates
3 pints/1½ litres white or light malt vinegar	7½ cups white or light malt vinegar
1 tablespoon coarse salt	1 tablespoon pickling salt
2 teaspoons mixed cake spice	2 teaspoons mixed cake spices
1 oz./25 g. mustard seeds	scant 3 tablespoons mustard seeds
½ oz./15 g. cloves	½ oz. cloves
½ teaspoon cayenne pepper	½ teaspoon cayenne
2 teaspoons ground ginger	2 teaspoons ground ginger
2 or 3 red chillis	2 or 3 chilis
2 blades mace	2 pieces mace
3 lb./1 kg. 400 g. soft brown sugar	3 lb. soft brown (Barbados) sugar
3 lb./1 kg. 400 g. stoned raisins	9 cups seeded raisins

Slice tomatoes, peel and core apples, peel and chop onions, stone and chop dates, and boil in the vinegar with the salt and spices until quite soft, pass through a nylon or hair sieve and put purée back in pan with the sugar and raisins (chopped or put through a mincer). Boil together for 45 minutes–1 hour, put into warm screw-top bottles, cork and screw down when cold.

Spicy Brown Sauce
steak sauce

Yield approx 1–1½ pints/6–9 dl./2½–3¾ cups

Imperial/Metric	American
1 lb./½ kg. shallots, chopped	1 lb. shallots, chopped
1 teaspoon black pepper	1 teaspoon black pepper
1 tablespoon black treacle	1 tablespoon molasses
1 teaspoon salt	1 teaspoon salt
1 clove of garlic, crushed	1 clove of garlic, crushed
¼ oz./8 g. chillis	¼ oz. chilis
1 tablespoon mushroom ketchup	1 tablespoon mushroom catsup
1 tablespoon anchovy paste	1 tablespoon anchovy paste
¼ oz./8 g. ground cloves	¼ oz. ground cloves
1 pint/6 dl. malt vinegar	2½ cups malt vinegar

Put all ingredients into a pan (except vinegar), and just cover with cold water, bring to the boil, and simmer until shallots are reduced to a pulp. Strain through a sieve, pressing well, then return to pan with vinegar, boil for 2–3 minutes and bottle. If a thicker sauce is liked, add ½ tablespoon cornflour mixed to a smooth paste with a little vinegar. This is not a long-keeping sauce, but can be kept for a few weeks.

Mint Sauce
for keeping

Yield approx ¾–1 pint/4½–6 dl./2–2½ cups

Imperial/Metric	American
½ pint/3 dl. vinegar	1¼ cups vinegar
6 oz./175 g. Demerara sugar	⅔ cup raw sugar
¼ pint/1½ dl. measure mint, freshly chopped	⅔ cup freshly chopped mint

Boil the vinegar and sugar together for a minute or so; make sure that the sugar is quite dissolved. Add the chopped mint, stir well and leave to go cold.

When cold, pour into glass-stoppered bottles if possible; otherwise use plastic-lined screw-tops. Don't use metal tops, for metal must not come in contact with vinegar. Dip the tops in melted wax for extra security, or put a strip of adhesive tape around the join between stoppers or screw-tops and the bottle itself. Add a little more vinegar when the sauce is required for use.

Lemon curd, Orange crush, see recipes, pages 17, 76

Spiced eggs

Preserving Eggs

Eggs for preserving should be new-laid, but not straight from the nest. Allow 24 hours for the temperature and air pressure inside the eggs to equalise; 1 to 2 days old, but not more than 3 days is the ideal age. Try to get thick-shelled eggs if possible; rough or unevenly shelled eggs should not be preserved. Do not wash the eggs as this makes the shells porous. If necessary, remove any soilings (from the nest) with a warm, damp cloth.

Preserving eggs in waterglass

Use a *new* galvanised pail, or stone crock if possible. A lid should be provided to keep out dust and to prevent loss of liquid through evaporation. Egg preserving pails can be bought in some districts.

To make the waterglass solution, follow the direction on the tin and three-quarters fill the container. When the solution is cold, add the eggs as they become available; it is not necessary to completely fill the container in one operation. Try to pack them with the pointed ends downwards; in this way it is more likely that the yolk will stay in the centre of the egg. The waterglass liquid should completely cover the eggs and more cold solution must be added as required.

Dry pickling eggs

It is possible to preserve eggs by coating the shells with oil, lard or butter, the idea being to exclude air from penetrating shells. This is a favourite country-woman's trick; she can be quite sure that her eggs are at the right age, as by this method, if the eggs were stale they would simply go bad, quite quickly, as the bacteria would be sealed inside the egg with its non-porous coating.

Nowadays, it is possible to buy a solution of fat into which the eggs are dipped (after wiping with a damp cloth), using tongs supplied with the solution. There is also a soft preparation that can be rubbed over the shells, but this is really just a variation of the country-woman's method. In any case the manufacturers' instructions should be followed.

After dipping or coating the eggs they should be left overnight to dry, then packed in boxes with partitions so that the eggs do not touch each other. The modern half-dozen egg boxes from the dairy or grocers' are ideal for the purpose. Store them in a cool, dry place until required.

Spiced Eggs

Yield approx 2-pint/1-litre/5-cup jar

Imperial/Metric	American
12 hard-boiled eggs	*12 hard-cooked eggs*
1½–2 pints/1 litre white vinegar	*3¾–5 cups white vinegar*
½ oz./15 g. root ginger, bruised	*½ oz. root ginger, bruised*
¼ oz./8 g. mustard seeds	*2 teaspoons mustard seeds*
¼ oz./8 g. white peppercorns	*¼ oz. white peppercorns*
2 chillis	*2 chilis*

After eggs have cooled, carefully remove the shells. Simmer the vinegar with the ginger, mustard seeds and peppercorns for 5 minutes; strain, and leave to cool. Arrange the eggs upright in a wide-mouthed jar; put the chillis on top. Completely cover with spiced vinegar. Tie down securely; keep for 2–3 weeks before using.

Note

The eggs should be boiled for 15–20 minutes to be sure they are thoroughly cooked. Brown spiced vinegar (see page 40) may be used, if liked, but it will slightly discolour the eggs.

Herb Vinegars

A very good and simple way of introducing the flavour of herbs to salad dressings, sauces, soups and stews is by using herb-flavoured vinegars. These are very simple to make, especially if you have a garden, or access to a garden where the herbs are grown. Mint and tarragon are the most usual herbs to choose, because of their aromatic flavour, but almost any herb such as sage, marjoram, thyme, basil, or a mixture of them, can be used.

Mint Vinegar

Yield approx 1 pint/6 dl./2½ cups

Imperial/Metric	American
1 pint/6 dl. white vinegar	2½ cups white vinegar
6 sprigs mint	6 sprigs mint
½ teaspoon castor sugar	½ teaspoon sugar

Put vinegar in a saucepan and bring to the boil. Wash mint, put 4 sprigs into the vinegar, first crushing them slightly between your fingers. Add sugar and stir well. *Immediately* the vinegar reaches boiling point, remove it from the heat. (Vinegar evaporates quickly, but it must be sterilised when it is to be added to any vegetable substance, or it will soon sour.)

Leave vinegar, with the mint still in it, to become quite cold. In the meantime, dry the remaining two sprigs of mint well, removing any faded leaves. Put the sprigs in a 1-pint (6-dl., 2½-cup) vinegar bottle, strain the vinegar into it and cover with a screw cap. The vinegar is ready for immediate use, but the mint flavour improves with keeping.

Tarragon, sage, marjoram, thyme and basil flavoured vinegars are made in the same way; a mixture of mint, tarragon and sage is very good.

Yogurt

Yogurt has been known for centuries by the peasant communities of the world but only since 1963, when the fruit-flavoured variety was introduced from Switzerland, has it become a popular part of our normal diet. It is basically milk with the addition of a fermenting agent, or baccilus, which produces lactic acid. This lactic acid aids digestion and the assimilation of calcium which makes it a valuable health food. The milk may be from the cow or the goat; it may be whole milk, skimmed, dried or evaporated, or a mixture of these. The nutritional value of the yogurt depends entirely on the milk chosen.

Natural yogurt has many uses in cooking – it can be stirred into soups, sauces, and casseroles, spooned over white fish before baking and used in salad dressings. It is expensive to buy in large quantities for a family, but it can be made at home for little more than the cost of the milk. The procedure is simple enough, although there are variations in the method of incubation. It is worthwhile testing each to see which produces the most satisfactory result or is the most convenient for yourself.

Yogurt

Imperial/Metric	American
1 pint/6 dl. milk	2½ cups milk
1 tablespoon natural yogurt or *yogurt culture	1 tablespoon unflavored yogurt or *yogurt culture

*This special culture is available from health stores, some chemists and dairies.

Method 1
Bring the milk to the boil and simmer for 1–2 minutes in order to thicken it. Pour into a bowl and set aside to cool to about 106°F./41°C. – hand-hot temperature – stirring frequently to prevent a skin forming, then stir in the natural yogurt or yogurt culture. Pour this mixture immediately into a warm, wide-necked vacuum flask, replace the top, and leave undisturbed for 8 hours, when it should be set. Store in the refrigerator.

Method 2
Bring the milk to the boil and simmer as in the previous method. Allow to cool and add the yogurt or culture, then pour into a warmed earthenware bowl. Cover with a clean cloth or with a piece of aluminium foil, then place in a warm airing cupboard or the warming drawer of a cooker until the milk has solidified.

Method 3
Proceed as for methods 1 and 2 until the yogurt or culture has been added. Now have ready 5 × 4-oz./125-g. wide-necked bottles, a biscuit tin, plastic foam, cotton wool, 1 cork mat and a table napkin. Line the sides and base of the tin with the plastic foam and lay the napkin in the tin with the ends hanging over the sides. Place the bottles in the prepared tin with spaces between, filling these spaces with cotton wool. Fill the bottles with the prepared milk mixture. Place the cork mat on top of the bottles, draw up the ends of the napkin and close the lid of the tin. Leave undisturbed for 8 hours at room temperature to obtain a good set. Once prepared, the tin need not be disturbed when removing the bottles, so that it is ready for use on future occasions.

Home Curing, Salting and Drying

Home Curing Hams and Bacon

The curing of bacon and hams is one of the oldest crafts in Britain; no countrywoman would have thought of being without one or two home-cured hams to 'cut at' when needed – throughout the year.

The methods of curing varied with each locality, and they were often closely guarded secrets. All sorts of homely herbs and flavourings were used and some used dry-salting and some brine-salting. Even the drying, or smoking of the hams differed, the simplest method being to hang the ham in the inglenook, or from hooks in the kitchen ceiling, leaving it to the smoke from the domestic fire, no matter what kind of wood was burning. A smoking with resinous wood, such as pine, was supposed to give a dark, fly-proof finish. Oak chips were considered the best for giving a mild smoky flavour. It is said that the original York hams were smoked with the oak sawdust collected during the building of York Minster; others say that the fine flavour and colour is due to the excellence of Yorkshire salt. Strictly speaking, a ham is the whole hind leg of a pig cut off round, at the joint, from the carcass, separately cured and allowed to mature. The gammon is the hind leg cut after the split carcass has matured in brine, and it is cut off square. The gammon, in turn, is often cut into smaller portions, usually three – gammon hock, middle gammon and corner gammon. The middle is the choicest cut and, of course, the most expensive; from it gammon rashers are cut. The hock and corner have the same flavour, but more bone, and the slices are more 'bitty' than the middle gammon; therefore they are cheaper. The overall price of a whole gammon makes it an economical buy. When you ask in the shop today for ready-cooked ham, you are almost certain to be offered boned-out middle or corner gammon which, technically speaking, is not ham. As it has usually been pressed and canned, it is difficult to tell its origin, but it is worth asking for Wiltshire gammon which is considered the best.

Pickled pork

The curing of pork to make it into ham or bacon is done in two stages. The first is salting and the second is the maturing by smoking; it is the maturing or smoking that gives the full flavour to cured pork, and enables it to be kept longer. Pork may, however, be preserved for some weeks by soaking in a pickle or weak solution of brine. The belly and flank, being thin joints, are the most suitable for salting, but any part can be treated in the same way, giving them longer time in the pickle.

A simple method of pickling is to cleanse the pork in a strong brine for 24 hours, the brine being made from

Greengage jam, Bramble and apple jelly, Plum wine, Bottled plums, see recipes, pages 10, 15, 28, 74

coarse salt (sea salt is best) and water, mixed strong enough to float an egg. This brine can be composed from 11 lb./5 kg. salt, 1 lb./½ kg. saltpetre and 4 gallons (18 litres, 5 gallons) water. It must be thoroughly boiled; scum will rise to the top of the water and this should be taken off until the liquid is quite clear. After soaking, the meat is taken out and is thoroughly cleansed from blood and other impurities by pressure with the hands. You now have pickled pork (or unsmoked bacon). It should be well dried and will keep some time in a cool, airy place and can be used as 'green bacon' or boiled in unsalted water, to eat hot or cold.

To cure ham or bacon

After the pickling process, and all the blood and other impurities have been squeezed out, the joint should be cured and smoked for longer keeping.

Simple Cure

Imperial/Metric	American
1 lb./450 g. soft brown sugar	1 lb. brown sugar
12 oz./350 g. coarse salt	1 cup pickling salt
1½ oz./40 g. saltpetre	1½ oz. saltpeter
10–12 lb./4½–5½ kg. ham or joint, pickled	10–12 lb. ham or joint, pickled
2 pints/generous litre malt vinegar	5 cups malt vinegar

Mix the sugar, salt and saltpetre together, rub mixture well into the pickled meat, put in a vessel big enough to hold it easily (a wooden tub is best) and sprinkle any remaining mixture over it. There should be a good layer of the curing mixture on top of the joint. Leave for 3 days, turning 2 or 3 times each day, then pour over the vinegar. Turn the joint in the brine every day for a month, then take it up, and rub all over with bran to dry.

Hang the joint high from a hook above but not too near the fire; it should be just close enough to come in contact with the smoky fumes. When it has been smoked for 3 to 4 weeks, cover it in strong muslin or put in a calico bag.

Wiltshire Cure

Imperial/Metric	American
10–12 lb./4½–5½ kg. ham, pickled (see page 62)	10–12 lb. ham, pickled (see page 62)
1 lb./450 g. common salt	1⅓ cups coarse salt
2 oz./50 g. saltpetre	2 oz. saltpeter
1 oz./25 g. prunella salt*	2 tablespoons prunella salt*
¼ oz./8 g. juniper berries	¼ oz. juniper berries
1 lb./450 g. dark treacle	1 lb. molasses
8 oz./225 g. bay salt*	⅔ cup bay salt*
½ oz./15 g. black pepper	½ oz. black pepper
2 pints/generous litre beer	5 cups beer

After pickling the ham put it in a deep vessel, wooden if possible. Boil all the remaining ingredients together, cool slightly then pour over the ham. Turn the ham daily for 1 month, making sure that all parts of the ham come in contact with the curing liquid; baste it with the liquid if necessary. Take up, dry well with a cloth, then cover with a cotton bag and hang high from the kitchen ceiling, near a wood fire. Hang and smoke for 5–6 weeks, inspecting frequently.

*Prunella salt and bay salt can be obtained from a chemist or herbalist.

Suffolk Sweet Cure

Imperial/Metric	American
10–12 lb./4½–5½ kg. ham, pickled (see page 62)	10–12 lb. ham, pickled (see page 62)
2 pints/generous litre beer	5 cups beer
1 lb./450 g. granulated sugar	2 cups sugar
1 lb./450 g. bay salt*	1⅓ cups bay salt*
½ oz./15 g. peppercorns	½ oz. peppercorns
2 pints/generous litre malt vinegar	5 cups malt vinegar
½ oz./15 g. saltpetre	½ oz. saltpeter
1 lb./450 g. coarse salt	1⅓ cups pickling salt
½ oz./15 g. whole cloves	½ oz. whole cloves
2 oz./50 g. hops	2 oz. hops
2 pints/generous litre water	5 cups water

*Bay salt can be obtained from a chemist or herbalist.

Dry the ham well after pickling. Boil all the ingredients together, except the ham, hops and water. Boil the hops in the water for 30 minutes, then strain into the other boiled ingredients. Put ham into a large fairly shallow dish. Pour the curing mixture over it. Leave for 5 to 6 weeks, basting with the curing liquid every day. Take it up, dab with a cloth to dry, then hang high up, near a wood fire until dry. Cover with a cotton bag and leave to smoke for 5 to 6 weeks, removing bag to inspect ham every week after the first month; do not allow it to become too dry.

Derbyshire Cure

Imperial/Metric	American
1 pint/6 dl. brown ale	*2½ cups brown ale*
1 pint/6 dl. stout	*2½ cups stout*
1 lb./450 g. dark treacle	*1 lb. dark treacle or molasses*
1 lb./450 g. coarse salt	*1⅓ cups pickling salt*
½ oz./15 g. saltpetre	*½ oz. saltpeter*
12–14 lb./5½–6½ kg. ham	*12–14 lb. ham*

Put all the ingredients, except the ham, in a large saucepan and boil for 5 minutes. If the ham has not already been pickled (see page 62), rub it all over with more coarse salt. Put it in a large curing tub. Pour the mixture in the saucepan over it while still hot. Keep the ham in the curing liquid for 3 weeks, turning and rubbing it every day. Take up, allow to drain, then put in a cotton bag, and hang up near a wood fire to dry and smoke for 3 to 4 weeks.

Preserving by Salting and Drying

Salting Beans

When you have a surplus of French or runner beans in the garden, or when there is a glut of them in the shops, it is a very good idea to preserve them by packing in salt in a jar. An unglazed, wide-necked earthenware jar is the best type, though large preserving jars can be used as long as care is taken that no salt comes in contact with metal lids. All jars should be wide-necked so that you can easily get your hand inside to press down the beans. It is not necessary to fill the jar completely at one go.

If you grow your own beans you will know that at the height of the season French and runner beans come to perfection day by day, quicker than you can use them up for daily cooking. When this happens, start salting the surplus. Natural coarse cooking salt, not the refined table kind, should be used. Table salt will cause scum to form on top of the beans, and the beans may go slimy. I have found that Malden crystallised sea salt is the 'saltiest' salt to use for this type of preserving. Allow 1 lb./½ kg. salt to every 3 lb./1½ kg. beans.

Wash, top and tail the beans; when tailing, start cutting from the thin edge of the beans, and pull the cut-away ends downwards on the thick side, so that any 'strings' that may have started to form will be pulled away. Over-ripe beans which have developed coarse strings should be discarded. Small French beans can be salted whole or snapped into pieces. Runner beans should be sliced.

Put a good layer of salt – about ½ inch/1 cm. deep – in the bottom of the jar. Put a layer of beans on top of the salt, about 1 inch/2½ cm. in depth, and continue with alternate layers until the jar is full, pressing each layer of beans down well. If you have not enough beans to fill the jar at one go, just sprinkle the top of the last layer of beans with salt, cover the jar with a plate, and continue the filling as the beans come along. Finish with a good layer of salt.

Cover the jar loosely with waxed paper and leave to stand for a few days. The beans will settle in the jar, leaving room for another layer, but be sure to finish off with a good layer of salt. Cover the jar closely with waxed paper – not metal lids – and store in a cool, dry, dark place. Putting the beans in a dark place helps to keep them a good colour, although they will darken slightly as time goes on.

To cook salted beans
Take out as many beans as are required, wash them well in cold water, and leave in cold water for one to two hours; if left for longer there is a risk that they will become slimy. Rinse again and cook in *unsalted* water until tender.

Storing Nuts in Salt

Filberts (hazelnuts) and walnuts can be kept in a fresh condition for several months, if perfectly ripe, dry and in good condition when gathered. Any loose outer husks should be removed and they should be scrubbed to remove any remnants of the soft outer shell; dry the nuts well after doing this. Pack nuts tightly in a wide-necked jar, leaving ½ inch/1 cm. clear at the top. Sprinkle coarse salt liberally among the nuts, tapping the jar on a table top to make the salt sift through the nuts. Cover the top ½ inch/1 cm. with salt, pressing down well.

Walnuts with imperfect shells are best shelled, the kernels spread out in a single layer on a baking sheet, and placed in a very cool oven (150°F./65°C., less than Gas Mark ¼) until dry, but not scorched. Allow the nuts to cool, then put them in a jar with a tight-fitting lid, sprinkle a little dry salt over them, cover, and store in a cool place.

Salted Almonds

Imperial/Metric	American
¼ pint/1½ dl. olive oil	⅔ cup olive oil
8 oz./225 g. blanched sweet almonds	1½ cups blanched sweet almonds
1 tablespoon celery salt or sea salt	1 tablespoon celery salt or sea salt
good sprinkling cayenne pepper	good sprinkling cayenne

Heat the oil in a wide, thick frying pan. Gently fry the nuts in the oil until biscuit-coloured, shaking the pan often; they should absorb most of the oil. Sprinkle in the salt and cayenne and stir the nuts well so they are evenly coated. Turn the nuts out on to a sheet of paper and toss them well so that all the loose salt drops off, and at the same time the nuts are evenly coated.

Allow to become quite cold before storing in waxed paper, or greaseproof paper bags, fastened with rubber bands so they are airtight.

The kernels of filberts (hazelnuts) or peanuts can be salted in the same way and make an excellent substitute for salted almonds.

Preserving by Drying

No special equipment is needed for drying vegetables, fruits and herbs. But you must be patient; the drying can take several days, or up to 8 hours in a very cool oven, set at the lowest temperature possible. A good place is on a slatted shelf in an airing cupboard, or along the edge of a shelf over a solid fuel cooker, but make sure that whatever is drying is covered loosely to keep off dust. If you grow herbs it is worthwhile drying some for winter use. Almost every garden has its mint patch for mint sauce during the summer; it is one of the most successful herbs for drying and makes excellent mint sauce when fresh mint is not available. Herbs for drying should be picked when they are in full leaf, and before flowering. They should be picked, after the dew has evaporated, on a dry, warm – not hot – day; hot sun is apt to extract the pungent flavour of the herbs.

Dried Plums

The purple plums are best for drying; they should be firm, but ripe and quite fresh. They are best dried whole, but if large can be cut in halves and the stones taken out. Cut plums should be dried with the cut sides uppermost to prevent the juice running out. Spread the plums on trays in a single layer, and dry slowly in a temperature between 100–150°F./40–65°C. If dried in an airing cupboard or oven, leave the door open slightly. If put into too high a temperature the skins harden before the pulp has had time to dry out and there is risk of the skins cracking. Dry until no moisture comes out when they are squeezed; this may take a day or two. Cool the fruit thoroughly, at room temperature, for several hours before storing. Pack in wooden or cardboard boxes lined with greaseproof paper, pressing the fruit down well, and store in a very dry place.

Dried Apricots

For drying, apricots should be fully ripe so that they can be halved without too much pressure on the fruit. Remove stones and proceed as for halved plums, though they will not take so long as the plums.

Dried peaches
Peaches are treated in the same way as apricots.

To cook dried stone fruits
Before cooking, all dried stone fruits should be soaked overnight in water to cover them, then stewed in the water in which they were soaked.

Dried apple rings

Dried Apple Rings

Firm, juicy, crisp apples should be used. Peel and core
the apples and cut them into rings about $\frac{1}{4}$ inch/$\frac{1}{2}$ cm.
thick. Make a weak brine solution by boiling 2 oz./50 g.
salt in 1 gallon (4$\frac{1}{2}$ litres, 10 pints) water and let it cool.
Drop the apple rings, as you cut them, into the solution
and leave for 5–8 minutes. Take them out and dry
them, by placing on thin rods or sticks, suspending
these across a baking dish or Yorkshire pudding tin, and
then putting them in a very cool oven (150°F., 65°C.,
less than Gas Mark $\frac{1}{4}$). The oven door should be left
open slightly to allow moisture to escape. Leave them to
dry until they resemble chamois leather in texture.
Allow to cool before putting into airtight tins or jars.

To cook dried apple rings

Soak dried apple rings in cold water for about 1 hour
before using, then stew, or cook in the usual way for
steamed puddings, pies and so on. A little of the water
in which they were soaked should be added to the
apples when cooking.

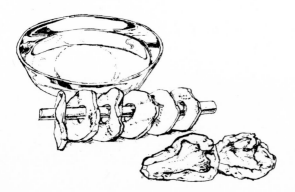

Dried Pears

Only dessert pears are suitable for drying and they
should be firm, but ripe. Peel thinly with a stainless
knife, cut in halves lengthwise and remove cores with a
sharp-edged spoon. The hard, pith-like piece leading
from the stalks should also be removed. As each pear is
prepared, drop it into a salt solution (1 tablespoon salt
to 12 pints/7 litres/15 pints water). Leave them for 5
minutes in the solution after all are prepared, placing a
plate on top to keep all the pears submerged.

Take up and drain. Arrange the pear halves cut sides
downwards on a wire cake-cooling tray with muslin
stretched over it, making one layer only. The pears can
be dried in an airing cupboard or in a very slow oven
(150°F./66°C., less than Gas Mark $\frac{1}{4}$). In either case
leave the door slightly open to allow moisture from the
fruit to escape.

The pears, when fully dried, should have a rubbery
texture and not be at all brown; the process will take
several hours.

Allow the pears to cool thoroughly before storing in an
airtight jar or tin.

To cook dried pears

Before cooking, pears need longer soaking than apples
and they can be left overnight without spoiling. Cook
them in the water in which they were soaked, adding
sugar just before cooking is finished.

Dried Herbs

Herbs, with the exception of parsley, do not need artificial heat to dry them. Sunshine, a warm kitchen or airing cupboard are most suitable. The usual, and most useful herbs for drying are thyme, tarragon, marjoram, sage, mint and bay leaves. Tie the herbs loosely in bunches, dip quickly in water, shake them, and hang them to dry where the air can circulate round. They should be protected from dust by putting them in thin paper bags or muslin squares. Strip the leaves from the stems when quite dry, and with the exception of bay leaves, which are kept whole, crush them with a rolling pin, as finely as possible. Store each herb separately in airtight tins or screw-top jars.

Dried parsley is dried quickly to keep it green. Wash bunches of parsley leaves in cold water, shake well and separate the leaves from the main stems. Spread leaves on a wire tray and dry them in a fairly hot oven (375°F., 190°C., Gas Mark 5) for a few minutes, watching them carefully, as the leaves brown quickly. When the parsley leaves are crisp, crush them and store as for other herbs, making sure that the parsley is quite cold before putting on the lids of tins or jars. Preferably store away from the light. The parsley stalks should also be included, as they have a lot of flavour although they will not crush as finely as the leaves.

Mixed herbs consist of powdered dried parsley, thyme and marjoram, in equal proportions, with double the quantity of powdered dried sage, and one or two crushed bay leaves.

Bouquet garni used for flavouring soups, stews, casseroles and stock consists of a teaspoonful mixed herbs with an extra bay leaf, a blade of mace, a sprig of parsley and three or four peppercorns all tied together in a piece of muslin. The bouquet is thrown away after its use in cooking. It is a good idea to make several bouquets garnis and keep them in an airtight container, so they are ready for use.

Dried Onion Rings

Choose medium-sized onions, peel them and cut into slices about ¼ inch/½ cm. thick. Separate the slices into rings; the very smallest centre rings are too small for drying and can be used at once for ordinary cooking. Plunge the bigger rings into fast boiling water and let them boil for half a minute, then strain in a colander and plunge them at once into cold water. Drain well and spread out on a cloth, to soak up the moisture. Spread them on a wire tray, such as is used for cooking cakes, and place in a very cool oven (no hotter than 150°F., 65°C., less than Gas Mark ¼) until the onions are quite crisp and dry. Leave the oven door slightly open to allow moisture to escape. The onion rings will discolour slightly but this is no detriment. Allow to cool, then store in an airtight jar.

To cook dried onion rings
When needed for cooking, soak the dried onion rings in warm water for 30 minutes.

Dried Peas

For the marrowfat type of peas the 'harvesting-off' method is the best. Leave the pods on the plants until they are quite dry and shrivelled, while the weather is dry. If wet weather sets in, pull up the plants when they begin to fade and the pods are dry, and leave them to dry in a cool, airy shed. When the pods are quite faded and papery, strip them off the plants, shell the peas, and spread them out on a tray in a warm place, such as over a solid fuel cooker or in an airing cupboard, with the door slightly open, until they are quite hard and dry. Put them in an airtight container when cold and cover tightly; store in a cool, dark place.

For young, sweet peas, the blanching method is the best. Shell the peas and tie in muslin; blanch them by plunging the bag in boiling water for 5 minutes, then dip in cold water. Drain them, turn out on to a dry towel and shake well to remove surface moisture. Spread them on trays in a single layer and dry very slowly in a very cool oven (150°F., 65°C., less than Gas Mark ¼) or in an airing cupboard, with the door left slightly open for moisture to escape.

Dried Beans

Haricot beans should be harvested and treated in the same way as marrowfat peas. Young French or runner beans should be prepared for cooking in the usual way, then blanched and dried as for young, sweet peas.

To cook dried peas and beans
Soak the required quantity in boiling water overnight,

adding a level teaspoon bicarbonate of soda to every 1 lb./½ kg. peas or beans. After soaking, strain and rinse, bring slowly to the boil in salted water and simmer until tender. This could take 50 minutes to 1 hour according to the variety and age of the peas or beans. They can be cooked in a pressure cooker, when they will take one-third of the usual time; the pressure cooker manufacturers' instructions should be followed carefully.

Dried Mushrooms

It is worth while drying any surplus mushrooms as they are so useful for making soups and flavouring stews, and after soaking they can be fried or grilled. In many Continental kitchens a string of dried mushrooms is always there, and the housewife just slips off one or two as she needs them, as we use a pinch of herbs. Dried mushrooms can be bought at some of the Continental stores in this country.

Mushrooms for drying must be fresh and well open; the button or half-closed kind are not really suitable. Remove the stems (these can be used in soups or stews) and peel the mushrooms if they are very dirty, but if they are clean, a wipe with a damp cloth is all that is necessary. Thread them on a fine string with a knot between each to prevent them touching and hang them to dry in a warm airy place. The edge of a kitchen shelf is quite good so long as no steam can get to them. Alternatively, you can suspend them on a rack in a very cool oven, (not more than 150°F., 66°C., less than Gas Mark ¼) with the oven door slightly open, or if you have a solid fuel cooker they can be placed over it. The mushrooms will become the texture of chamois leather. They can be stored in a jar in a dry place or if you are going to use them frequently they can hang in the kitchen, so long as they are free from dust and steam.

To cook dried mushrooms

When wanted to flavour stews, casseroles, or soups, just break off as many as you require, and put them straight into whatever you are making. For frying or grilling, soak them in a little cold water, or if wanted quickly, put in a steamer for a few minutes. Dry them well before putting in a frying pan or under the grill.

General instructions for storing dried foods

All dried fruits and vegetables must be absolutely cold before being put into jars or boxes with tightly fitting lids. Store these in a dry, airy, preferably dark place; light causes vegetables to change colour. If mould forms during storage it means that the vegetables or fruits were not absolutely dry before storing, or that your storage place is warm or damp. If the vegetables or fruits are used *at once* at the first sign of mould, there are no dangers to health, but if there is a definite musty or sour smell it is risky to use them.

Put dried herbs into small tins with tight-fitting lids and store in a dark place; they lose aroma if kept in paper bags or exposed to the air.

Home Freezing

Home freezing is one of the most satisfactory and popular methods of food preservation today, particularly in country areas where fruits, vegetables, poultry and game are often readily available in prime condition for only short periods of the year.

It is not possible to cover the subject adequately in the scope of this book, but there are several books giving a comprehensive coverage which will see anyone through the problems of buying and using a freezer. The avoidance of waste in times of glut, the convenience of having a reserve of food and the enjoyment of eating out-of-season foods, more than justify the cost of the special freezer cabinet. When cooking, the 'make two and freeze one' method saves time, labour and fuel, and prevents wastage of ingredients and money, so the long-term economy of preserving foods by freezing must be offset against the capital outlay.

Full instructions for home freezing are usually supplied in a booklet issued with the deep freezer cabinet, but for more detailed advice it is worthwhile consulting a book devoted entirely to this subject.

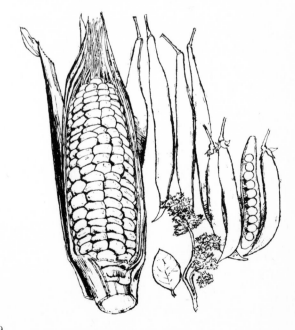

Home-Made Wines and Beers

The making of wines, ales and beers was once as important a part of the country-woman's yearly round of kitchen tasks as the making of jams, pickles and other preserves; no Christmas was complete without its bottles of damson, elderberry or rhubarb wine, made the previous summer. Or better still, made the summer before that, because the older the wine, the better it is.

War-time sugar rationing halted home-made wine-making, for though you might generally economise on sugar, you can't in wine-making, and there is no substitute for it.

But now that men have taken up wine-making as a hobby, there is a real revival of interest. The simple, homely methods, old family secrets or tricks of the trade, if not exactly frowned upon, are often regarded as *too* simple and many of today's wine-makers feel much happier with the gadgetry and chemical ingredients that come with 'do-it-yourself' wine-making outfits. However, the process of wine-making remains basically the same, and there is no need for any special equipment.

Utensils

Where the pressing and mashing method is used, a large earthenware bowl or panshon, wooden tub or even a washstand basin, will do. For pressing fruits, use a large wooden spoon, a meat beater, or vegetable masher. The wine (at this stage it is called the 'must') stays in the bowl, well covered, for several days to allow first stages of fermentation to take place. Then it is put in the final fermentation container.

When cooking is necessary, any large thick aluminium pan can be used. Another large earthenware bowl is needed to hold the 'must' during the first fermentation and a cask or jar in which the wine will remain, loosely corked, until fermentation is complete. Then a funnel for bottling (glass, *never* metal), a hair or nylon sieve, or a nylon conical-shaped gravy or sauce strainer, muslin squares, filter paper such as those used for filtering coffee – and that's about all. Except, of course, dry sterilised bottles – clear for light-coloured wines, dark green for red wines – with new corks for the final bottling and some labels to show the name of the wine and the date of making.

Nothing metal must come into contact with the wine during preparation and fermentation.

The wine cask

If you are new to wine-making, I suggest that you start with a small quantity, say a gallon, for which you do not need a wine cask. A wine cask is an advantage, as it has a tap which makes it easier to draw off the wine into bottles after fermentation, but I have made many a gallon of wine using a stone or glass wine jar – the kind with two little round handles at the top for lifting.

A new cask should be soaked in salty water before the wine is put into it to ferment; a used cask should be soaked in plain water. The cask must be absolutely clean; scald it with lots of boiling water with a little soda added. Rinse it well, and examine the inside with an electric torch, to be sure no stray bits and pieces have been left behind. I have heard of a whole brewing of wine being ruined by a piece of cork left behind in the cask.

Ingredients

Almost everything that grows can be made into wines – roots, fruit, flowers, herbs, leaves; even things which we usually call waste have their uses – skins of oranges and lemons, windfall apples and pears, apple and pear peelings and cores left over when making jam or bottling, under-sized gooseberries and currants, mis-shapen parsnips and beetroot. And the toughest rhubarb is the best for rhubarb wine.

Soft water is best for wine-making; if you live in a hard-water district, and have no access to spring water, it is best to boil the water first and let it go cold before using it.

White, granulated or crystallised sugar should always be used for light-coloured wines, and Demerara helps to give a good colour to dark wines, such as beetroot, damson, orange, rhubarb, bilberry. Never use moist brown sugar – and never try to economise on sugar: 3–4 lb./$1\frac{1}{2}$–$1\frac{3}{4}$ kg. to the gallon ($4\frac{1}{2}$ litres, 10 pints) is usual; some wines need more.

You'll notice that yeast is often mentioned as an ingredient. This is necessary to help convert the sugar in the fruit, and the added sugar, into alcohol. Very few fruits (grapes are an exception) contain enough natural sugar to do this without the help of the yeast ferment. Fresh fruits have a bloom on their skins; this is natural yeast, but most of it is lost in washing and preparing the fruit. Root vegetables have none of this natural yeast, so yeast is always used to start fermentation, usually by spreading it on toasted bread. The toast acts as a a nutrient or fertiliser for the yeast and helps fermentation start quickly. Some people are fussy about using the right kind of 'wine' yeast, but ordinary baker's yeast, or brewer's yeast if you can get it, seems to make a good job of it. Dried yeast can be used, but it must be reconstituted in the correct proportions given in the instructions. Remember that only half as much dried yeast is used, so halve the weight of fresh yeast given in a recipe.

Additives

Keen wine-makers like to experiment to get different flavour or 'zing' to their brews. Some say that the addition of cloves, preserved ginger, whole allspice, peppercorns or mustard seeds give a whisky-like flavour, while adding wheat, barley, raisins or sultanas, vine leaves, hops and malt, is said, by others, to be an improvement. But I do advise you to experiment carefully only *after* you have reached something like perfection with the basic recipes.

For my part, I would prefer to keep the smoothness and natural bouquet of the wine, and rely on long keeping to give it potency and 'body'. My exception to this is a little acid in the form of lemon juice, added to flower and some root wines, as these are lacking in natural acidity. A small amount of brandy or whisky, added after fermentation, can't do anything but improve the quality of any wine, but it is not essential. Large sultanas, which are, after all, a form of grape, give a pleasant flavour – not more than three in each bottle before final corking. When the addition of orange or lemon peel is required, use only the thinly-pared yellow part; the white part contains pectin, which causes pectin haze in the wine and is very difficult, almost impossible, to get rid of. Left-over orange or lemon peel can be added to the wine.

Fermentation

It is essential that fermentation of the 'must' should begin quickly; if it is slow in starting, the wine will have a sour, vinegary taste. Wine that is bottled before final fermentation is complete will be cloudy; take care not to tightly cork the wine while fermentation is still taking place, or the bottles will explode and you will lose your wine.

After the preparation of the 'must' – that is, the cooked or crushed fruit, vegetables or flowers, water, sugar and yeast (when used) – the bowl must be kept in an even, warm temperature, around 70°F./21°C. A warm kitchen or heated greenhouse is suitable. The bowl must be well covered; a piece of flannel or old blanket is ideal as this is 'cosy', and aids fermentation; it also keeps out the air.

After the wine has been strained into the cask or jar for final fermentation, it must be kept filled to the brim. A little of the wine being fermented should be kept back to replace that lost in fermentation. This is to prevent air getting into the wine and making it sour; if a towel or piece of muslin is also placed over the bung hole or top of the jar it will help to exclude air.

A fermentation lock simplifies the process, and makes quite certain that fermentation is complete. It costs very little and comes complete with a cork that fits into the standard wine jar (see colour picture page 63). The cork excludes all air, thus keeping out any bacteria that would sour the wine, and yet fermentation bubbles are passed up into the lock and can easily be removed. This process is repeated until no fermenting wine passes into it. When fermentation has ceased – that is, when there is no sign of frothing and no hissing sound coming from the cask or jar, or the fermentation lock is clear – the

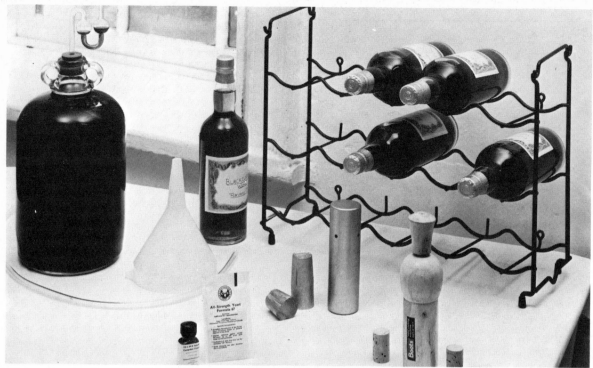

Wine making, bottling and corking equipment

wine is strained again. Strain through a hair or nylon sieve with two or three layers of filter paper lining it, then the wine can be bottled. This straining and filtering may sound tedious, but it is essential if you are to get a clear, brilliant wine. Even after this has been done, the wine must be left to clear itself in its own time, but that time can be shortened if you strain and filter thoroughly. And don't forget – *never* cork tightly until you are quite sure that all 'working' has ceased.

Clearing and fining

If, in spite of all your care, you find that the wine is cloudy, you will have to help in the clearing and fining of it.

Most wines clear naturally, and you must be patient and not be tempted to try your brew without giving it several months to do this. It is said that the hardest part of home wine-making is the waiting before you drink it! There are three ways in which you can clear the wine:

1 Fresh and absolutely clean egg shells are crushed and sprinkled into the wine – use 4 shells to each gallon ($4\frac{1}{2}$ litres, 10 pints). The only drawback is that this method is apt to take colour from the wine, though the flavour is not affected. But if you *want* white wine, then use egg shells to clear it. When clear, strain into clean bottles.

2 Beat 1 egg white in a pint (6 dl., $2\frac{1}{2}$ cups) wine, and pour carefully into the wine to be cleared. As the beaten

egg white sinks to the bottom of the bottle, it carries the hazy substances with it. This quantity of egg white and wine will clear several pints of wine. Strain off the cleared wine into clean bottles, cork securely and let it 'rest' a while, before drinking it.

3 The simplest way of clearing and fining wine is to use isinglass. This is a light, very fine form of gelatine, like candyfloss in appearance. It can be bought at the chemists and you can get quite a quantity in 1 oz./25 g. Put a pinch of it (roughly the size of a large walnut) in each bottle. It then swells and works up and down the bottle, transforming the haze into a sediment. Soon there will be brilliantly clear wine on top of the sediment, and you can strain it off into clean bottles. You will lose some of the wine in clearing it, but in the long run there is less loss than if you left sediment in the bottles; you would have to throw away the bottoms anyway, and then not be sure of getting a really sparkling glass of wine.

The yield from each recipe is approximately equal to the quantity of liquid given in the recipe – that is, if the recipe calls for 1 gallon/$4\frac{1}{2}$ litres/10 pints of water, you will get roughly the same amount of wine. However, allowance must be made for loss during fermentation and straining; though in the case of fruit wines, the juice extracted from the fruit will be added to the liquid content, and in many cases will offset this loss.

Apple Wine

Imperial/Metric	American
6 lb./3 kg. apples (windfalls will do if bruises are removed)	6 lb. apples (windfalls will do if bruises are removed)
4 oz./125 g. barley	¼ lb. barley
4 oz./125 g. sultanas	¾ cup sultanas
1 gallon/4¾ litres water	1¼ gallons water
rind and juice of 1 lemon	rind and juice of 1 lemon
4 lb./2 kg. Demerara sugar	4 lb. raw sugar

Chop apples into small pieces, put into a large bowl, add barley and sultanas and the water, rind and juice of lemon. Stir and press the apples every day for 3 weeks. Strain through a jelly bag or muslin into another bowl already containing the sugar, stir until sugar dissolves, cover with cloth and leave in warm place for 3 weeks until scum rises. Skim, pour through funnel into a 1-gallon/4¾-litre/10-pint stone jar up to the brim, cork loosely until fermentation ceases. Keep the jar topped up with a little surplus liquid. Pour into bottles through a funnel with filter paper inside; avoid pouring in sediment. Cork lightly and leave for 6 months at least.

Pouring fermented liquid into stone jar

Apple and Bilberry Wine

Imperial/Metric	American
6 lb./3 kg. apples (windfalls will do if bruises are removed)	6 lb. apples (windfalls will do if bruises are removed)
1 gallon/4¾ litres water	1¼ gallons water
4 lb./2 kg. bilberries	4 lb. bilberries
8 oz./225 g. raisins or sultanas	1½ cups raisins or seedless white raisins
4 lb./2 kg. sugar	4 lb. sugar

Chop apples, rejecting bruises, but do not peel or core. Put them in an earthenware bowl with half the water; stir and press them for a week, then strain. Three days after you have put the apples in the water, cover the bilberries with the rest of the water, leave for 4 days, then squeeze well and strain.

Combine the liquids. Add chopped raisins and sugar and stir until sugar dissolves. Cover and leave to ferment for 3 weeks, skim, strain into a gallon jar, corking loosely until fermentation has quite ceased. Bung tightly and after 6 months rack off (gently pour the wine off, leaving sediment undisturbed) into bottles. Cork tightly and leave undisturbed for 6 months.

This is a 'port wine' type of wine, and when made from wild bilberries is a great favourite in the North.

Rhubarb Wine

Yield approx 1 gallon/4¾ litres

Imperial/Metric	American
6 lb./3 kg. red rhubarb	6 lb. red rhubarb
1 gallon/4¾ litres cold water	1¼ gallons cold water
4 lb./2 kg. Demerara sugar	4 lb. raw sugar
juice and rind of 1 lemon	juice and rind of 1 lemon
4 oz./125 g. raisins	⅔ cup raisins
1 oz./25 g. fresh yeast on slice of toast	1 cake compressed yeast on slice of toast
¼ oz./8 g. isinglass	¼ oz. isinglass

Wipe rhubarb and cut into small pieces, put into bowl and cover with the water. Leave for 2 weeks, covered, stirring every day and crushing the rhubarb well. Strain and squeeze through wide-meshed strainer. Throw away pulp.

Strain the liquor through muslin or jelly bag, then warm it and add the sugar, stirring until dissolved. Add finely peeled yellow lemon rind and juice and the cut-up raisins. Add yeast on toast. Leave to ferment for a week to 10 days, stirring often. Skim and pour into cask or jar, adding the isinglass. Bung or cork loosely until all frothing stops, then secure cork or bung and leave for 6 months. Bottle and leave for another 3 months.

Blackcurrant Wine

Imperial/Metric	American
1 gallon/4¾ litres blackcurrants	1¼ gallons black currants
1 gallon/4¾ litres water	1¼ gallons water
4 lb./1¾ kg. sugar	4 lb. sugar
2 slices lightly toasted bread	2 slices lightly toasted bread
1 oz./25 g. fresh yeast	1 cake compressed yeast

Put the blackcurrants and the water together and bring to the boil slowly, and simmer until all the goodness is in the water (about 20 minutes). Then strain. Put the sugar and 1 slice of lightly toasted bread into a bowl. Pour the boiling blackcurrant liquid over and stir until the sugar is dissolved. When lukewarm add the yeast spread on the remaining slice of toast and ferment 14 days. Strain and pour into cask, corking loosely, until fermentation stops, then strain, bottle and cork tightly. Keep 1 or 2 years.

Elderberry Wine

Imperial/Metric	American
4 lb./2 kg. ripe elderberries	4 lb. ripe elderberries
1 gallon/4¾ litres water	1¼ gallons water
3 lb./1½ kg. sugar	3 lb. sugar
8 oz./225 g. raisins	½ lb. raisins
1 oz./25 g. fresh yeast on slice of toast	1 cake compressed yeast on slice of toast

Strip berries from stalks. Boil in the water for 10 minutes. Strain, add sugar to liquid with the chopped raisins and simmer 20 minutes. Let it cool in bowl then add yeast spread on toast, leave to ferment 3 weeks, then skim and strain into stone jar. Cork loosely until fermentation ceases, then tighten cork; keep for 6–9 months.

Gooseberry Wine

Imperial/Metric	American
4 lb./2 kg. gooseberries	4 lb. gooseberries
1 gallon/4¾ litres water	1¼ gallons water
3–4 lb./1½–2 kg. sugar to each 1 gallon/4¾ litres juice (depending on sweetness of berries)	3–4 lb. sugar to each 1¼ gallons juice (depending on sweetness of berries)

The gooseberries should be green, but not hard. Bruise well and put into earthenware bowl, add water and mix and mash well. Leave covered for 4 days, stirring and pressing fruit well every day. Strain and measure liquid. Return this, with the right proportion of sugar, into the bowl, and stir until sugar dissolves. Pour into cask or

stone jar and leave in warm place until fermentation ceases, 2–3 weeks. Cork lightly until frothing stops, then tighten corks. Bottle in 6 months, putting one or two raisins in each bottle.

Keep for 3 months.

Plum or Damson Wine

Imperial/Metric	American
4 lb./2 kg. red plums or damsons	4 lb. red plums or damsons
1 gallon/4¾ litres boiling water	1¼ gallons boiling water
½ oz./15 g. stick cinnamon	½ oz. stick cinnamon
4 lb./2 kg. sugar	4 lb. sugar
1 oz./25 g. fresh yeast on slice of toast	1 cake compressed yeast on slice of toast

Wipe and prick the plums or damsons and pour the boiling water over them. Add cinnamon, cover and leave for 4 days, stirring every day and crushing fruit. Strain, add sugar and stir until dissolved. Strain again through flannel or filter paper, add yeast on toast, cover and leave to ferment for 14 days. Skim and pour into cask or jar, bung lightly until frothing ceases, then bung tightly. Leave for 6 months, then bottle. Cork tightly and leave at least 3 months.

Shown in colour on page 63

Parsnip Wine

Imperial/Metric	American
5 lb./2¼ kg. parsnips	5 lb. parsnips
1 gallon/4¾ litres water	1¼ gallons water
4 lb./1¾ kg. sugar	4 lb. sugar
1 oz./25 g. bruised root ginger	1 oz. bruised root ginger
juice and rind of 1 lemon	juice and rind of 1 lemon
1 oz./25 g. yeast on slice of toast	1 cake compressed yeast on slice of toast

Peel and wash parsnips, cut them up and boil in the water until tender. Stir and press well, then strain through a jelly bag. Add the sugar and bruised root ginger and boil until sugar has dissolved. Pour into a bowl and add lemon juice and rind (yellow part only) and the chopped raisins. Cool and add yeast spread on toast. Cover with teatowel and leave for 14 days, removing scum as it rises. Strain into cask or jar. Bung or cork tightly when fermentation ceases, leave for 6 months, then bottle and leave for another 3 months.

Grape Wine

Imperial/Metric	American
6 lb./2¾ kg. grapes (any kind)	6 lb. grapes (any kind)
1 gallon/4¾ litres water	1¼ gallons water
3½ lb./1 kg. 600 g. white sugar	3½ lb. sugar
¼ pint/1½ dl. boiling water	⅔ cup boiling water

Bruise each grape between finger and thumb, cover with cold water. Stir and press the grapes each day for 7 days, then strain, throwing away the pulp. Strain a second time through a clean teatowel. Add sugar and stir until it is dissolved, then add the boiling water and set the wine in a warm place to ferment. When fermented 14 days, skim and bottle, corking lightly until all hissing ceases.

Black Grape Wine

Imperial/Metric	American
3 lb./1½ kg. black grapes	3 lb. purple grapes
1 gallon/4¾ litres cold water	1¼ gallons cold water
3 lb./1½ kg. sugar	3 lb. sugar

Put the grapes in a bowl and crush them. Cover with the cold water. Stand for 5 days, stirring several times each day, then strain. Add the sugar, stir until it dissolves and set in a warm place to ferment (see Fermentation, page 71). Leave 10 days, then strain and bottle, but do not cork until all signs of fermentation have ceased (see Utensils, page 70).

Keep for at least 6 months before using.

Ginger Wine

Imperial/Metric	American
⅛ oz./4 g. essence of ginger	⅛ oz. essence of ginger
⅛ oz./4 g. essence of capsicum	⅛ oz. essence of capsicum
½ oz./15 g. burnt sugar	½ oz. burnt sugar
rind and juice of 3 lemons	rind and juice of 3 lemons
4 pints/2¼ litres water	10 cups (5 pints) water
2 lb./900 g. granulated sugar	2 lb. sugar
½ oz./15 g. tartaric acid	½ oz. tartaric acid

A chemist will put the first three ingredients in a bottle for you. Pare lemon rind thinly, simmer in water for a few minutes. Put sugar, lemon juice and tartaric acid in large bowl, add boiling water and lemon rinds. Stir until sugar is dissolved, cool. Add ingredients in bottle, mix well. Remove rinds, bottle and cork tightly.

Ready to drink in a few days, but is better when allowed to mature. It keeps indefinitely.

Dandelion Wine

Imperial/Metric	American
3 quarts/3½ litres dandelion flower heads	7½ pints (15 cups) dandelion flower heads
1 gallon/4¾ litres boiling water	1¼ gallons boiling water
rind and juice of 1 lemon and 1 orange	rind and juice of 1 lemon and 1 orange
3 lb./1½ kg. white sugar	3 lb. sugar
1 inch/2½ cm. bruised root ginger	1 inch bruised root ginger
1 oz. fresh yeast on slice of toast	1 cake compressed yeast on slice of toast

Wash flowers, put in bowl, cover with boiling water, cover and leave for 3 days, stirring every day. Squeeze flowers out, put liquid in pan with the rind, yellow parts only, and juice of lemon and orange, sugar and ginger, and boil for 30 minutes. Pour into bowl and leave to cool, then add the yeast on toast. Leave to ferment for 6 days, strain into jar or cask, bunging lightly until fermentation ceases, then tighten bung and leave for 6 months. Bottle, cork lightly and leave another 3 months.

A few raisins added to each bottle is an improvement, but if you do this, do not cork tightly for a little while in case the raisins set up more fermentation.

Marigold Wine

Imperial/Metric	American
1-quart/good 1-litre measure marigold flowers	5 cups marigold flowers
1 gallon/4¾ litres water	1¼ gallons water
3 lb./1½ kg. sugar	3 lb. sugar
2 lemons	2 lemons
8 oz./225 g. raisins	1½ cups raisins
8 oz./225 g. honey	⅔ cup honey
½ oz./15 g. fresh yeast on slice of toast	½ cake compressed yeast on slice of toast

The flowers should be gathered on a dry day. Cover them with the water and leave for a week, stirring each day. Then strain through fine strainer. Throw away pulp. Add to the liquid the sugar, sliced lemons, chopped raisins and honey, and on top of this float toast spread with yeast; cover and leave to ferment for 3 weeks.

Skim, strain into jar or cask, cork lightly until all fermentation ceases, then tighten cork and leave for 6 months. Bottle, cork well and leave for 3 months.

Beetroot Wine

Imperial/Metric	American
4 lb./2 kg. beetroot, washed and chopped	4 lb. beets, washed and chopped
1 gallon/4¾ litres water	1¼ gallons water
½ oz./15 g. cloves	½ oz. cloves
1 oz./25 g. root ginger	1 oz. root ginger
4 lb./2 kg. sugar	4 lb. sugar
juice of 1 lemon	juice of 1 lemon
1 oz./25 g. fresh yeast on slice of toast	1 cake compressed yeast on slice of toast

Quickly chop the beetroot into the water, add cloves and ginger and cook until tender, about 20 minutes. Strain, add sugar and lemon juice while liquid is still hot, stir until sugar dissolves, then add the yeast on toast. Let it ferment for 3 weeks. Skim, strain into stone jar, bung loosely until there is no sign of froth, then tighten bung. Leave for 6 months, then bottle, cork tightly and leave for another 6 months.

Note

A little brandy added after fermentation is an improvement, but it remains a good wine without this additive.

Potato Wine

Imperial/Metric	American
2 lb./1 kg. potatoes	2 lb. potatoes
1 gallon/4¾ litres water	1¼ gallons water
juice and rind of 1 orange and 1 lemon	juice and rind of 1 orange and 1 lemon
8 oz./225 g. wheat	½ lb. wheat
3 lb./1½ kg. sugar	3 lb. sugar
8 oz./225 g. raisins	1½ cups raisins
½ oz./15 g. fresh yeast	½ cake compressed yeast

Wash and peel potatoes and cook gently in the water until soft. Strain the water on to the lemon and orange rinds and juices, add the wheat, sugar and raisins. When the liquid has cooled a little, add the yeast, creamed with a little sugar. Cover bowl with towel and leave in warm place for 3 weeks, stirring often. Then filter into cask or jar; bung loosely. When fermentation stops, tighten bung and leave for 6 months before bottling.

This wine becomes very potent when kept several months.

Elderflower Champagne

Imperial/Metric	American
1 pint/6 dl. measure fully-blown elderflowers, plucked free from green parts	2½ cups full-blown elderflowers, plucked free from green parts
1 gallon/4¾ litres water	1¼ gallons water
3½ lb./1 kg. 600 g. white sugar	3½ lb. sugar
1 lb./450 g. split stoned raisins	1 lb. split, seeded raisins
juice of 1 lemon	juice of 1 lemon
1 oz./25 g. fresh yeast	1 cake compressed yeast

Put the flowers in a pan with the water and simmer for 15 minutes. Pour into a bowl, add sugar, raisins and lemon juice. Stir until sugar is dissolved, and when lukewarm sprinkle the yeast on top. Stir once a day for 14 days, then remove scum and strain into a clean, dry stone jar, being careful not to disturb any sediment. Cork loosely, and when wine has finished fermenting, cork very tightly. Bottle in 6 months, straining through flannel or filter paper, and cork tightly with sterilised corks. Leave for 3 months.

Prune and Cherry Port

Imperial/Metric	American
2 lb./1 kg. prunes	2 lb. prunes
1 gallon/4¾ litres water	1¼ gallons water
2 lb./1 kg. black cherries	2 lb. black cherries
4 lb./2 kg. sugar	4 lb. sugar
1 oz./25 g. fresh yeast	1 cake compressed yeast
slice of toast	slice of toast

Soak the prunes in the water overnight. Simmer until very tender. Add the cherries to the prunes and squeeze and stir every day for 10 days. Then press out all liquid from the pulp, which you throw away. Add the sugar to the liquid and stir until it dissolves. Add the yeast spread on both sides of the toast, then leave to ferment for 16 days (see Fermentation, page 71). Skim, strain and bottle, but do not cork until all fermentation bubbles have ceased.

Keep for at least 6 months.

Orange Crush

Imperial/Metric	American
1½ lb./700 g. granulated sugar	1½ lb. sugar
1 oz./25 g. citric acid	1 oz. citric acid
rind (orange part only) and juice of 4 large oranges	rind (orange part only) and juice of 4 large oranges
1 quart/1¼ litres boiling water	5 cups boiling water

Put the sugar, citric acid, orange juice and thinly peeled rind in a saucepan, pour on the boiling water, stir over low heat until sugar dissolves. Bring just to boiling point. Strain and leave to cool. Pour into dry sterilised bottles. Cork tightly. To serve, use 1½–2 tablespoons to a tumbler of water.

For **Lemon Crush** substitute 4 lemons for the oranges and increase the amount of sugar to 2 lb./1 kg.

Shown in colour on page 59

Home-Brewed Beer

With beer the price it is, it is not surprising that men who like their pint – or pints! – have turned their hands to making their own beer. It is all so simple and quick to do; in three hours you can make 5 gallons (23 litres, 6¼ gallons) of good, fairly strong beer, in your own kitchen at a very low cost per pint. And in three weeks you can drink the beer.

Equipment? Simple: 20 1-quart (1¼-litre, 5-cup) bottles, which your local pub or off-licence will let you have for a few pence; one 5-gallon (23-litre, 6¼-gallon) plastic dustbin (a well-known store sells them at a very reasonable price); a length of tube for syphoning the beer, though it can be poured into the bottles; a 5-pint (3-litre, 6½-pint) saucepan for boiling the hops. A useful thing to have is a hydrometer – a glass tube with a narrow neck and bulbous end, marked off in graduated degrees – which when placed on top of the fermenting beer shows when the fermentation is complete. But experienced beer-makers have learned to rely on their own judgment, and are apt to scorn such 'new-fangled' ideas.

Beer

To fill 20 1-quart/1¼ litre/5-cup bottles

Imperial/Metric	American
4 oz./125 g. hops	*¼ lb. hops*
water	*water*
2 lb./1 kg. Demerara sugar	*2 lb. raw sugar*
1 tablespoon black treacle	*1 tablespoon dark treacle or molasses*
4 lb./2 kg. malt extract	*4 lb. malt extract*
1 oz./25 g. fresh baker's yeast	*1 cake compressed yeast*
20 small lumps sugar	*20 small cubes sugar*

Put hops in muslin bag and tie securely. Simmer for 45 minutes in 4 pints (2¼ litres, 5 pints) water. Throw away spent hops. Dissolve the sugar in 2 pints (1¼ litres, 5 cups) hot water, add the treacle and stir until well blended. Mix with the hop infusion.

Pour all into a well scalded 5-gallon (23-litre, 6¼-gallon) bin, and while still hot add the malt. Make up to 5 gallons (23 litres, 6¼ gallons) by adding cold or warm water until the final temperature is blood heat. Sprinkle yeast on top. Stand off the ground in a warm place. Fermentation will start in about 24 hours, and will be completed in 6–8 days. If using a hydrometer, float it on top; when it registers between 1,000 and 1,010, fermentation is complete.

Syphon or pour into well-cleaned bottles. Put 1 lump sugar in each 1-quart (1¼-litre, 5-cup) bottle, or ½ lump in 1-pint (6-dl., 2½-cup) bottles. Cork or screw down tightly, and leave in cool place 2–3 weeks, or until beer has cleared completely.

Mild Ale

Imperial/Metric	American
6 oz./175 g. hops	*6 oz. hops*
8 gallons/36 litres water	*10 gallons water*
3 lb./1½ kg. Demerara sugar	*3 lb. raw sugar*
2 oz./50 g. fresh yeast	*2 cakes compressed yeast*

Boil the hops and water gently for 45 minutes, strain over the sugar, allow to cool, then add the yeast. Leave to ferment for 5 days, then cask or bottle. It will be ready for use when it has settled.

Hop Beer

Imperial/Metric	American
10 oz./275 g. hops	*10 oz. hops*
1 oz./25 g. bruised root ginger	*1 oz. bruised root ginger*
8 gallons/36 litres water	*10 gallons water*
6 lb./2¾ kg. brown sugar	*6 lb. brown sugar*
4 oz./125 g. fresh yeast	*4 cakes compressed yeast*
1 slice burnt toast	*1 slice scorched toast*

Boil the hops and ginger in the water for 1 hour, then strain on to the sugar in a bowl, or wooden tub, if possible. When lukewarm add the yeast spread on a slice of burnt toast. Let it work for 3–4 days, then bottle and tie down securely. Ready in 2–3 weeks.

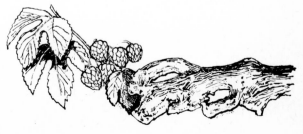

Nettle Beer

Imperial/Metric	American
1 gallon/4¾ litres young nettles	1¼ gallons young nettles
1 gallon/4¾ litres water	1¼ gallons water
½ oz./15 g. root ginger	½ oz. root ginger
1 oz./25 g. hops	1 oz. hops
1 lemon	1 lemon
1 lb./450 g. sugar	1 lb. sugar
1 oz./25 g. cream of tartar	1 oz. cream of tartar
1 oz./25 g. fresh yeast	1 cake compressed yeast

Wash nettles and put into a saucepan with water, ginger, hops and cut-up lemon. Boil for 15 minutes. Put sugar and cream of tartar in a large bowl, strain nettle mixture on to it, and stir until sugar has dissolved. Cream the yeast with a little sugar and add. Leave for 12 hours, or longer, until yeast rises to the top. Skim and then pour into bottles. Cork and tie down securely.

It can be used at once. In summer time when the beer was always wanted, it was the habit of country people to serve it in a jug, straight from the bowl, not bothering to bottle it at all.

Ginger Beer

Imperial/Metric	American
2 lemons	2 lemons
1½ lb./700 g. sugar	1½ lb. sugar
1 oz./25 g. bruised root ginger	1 oz. bruised root ginger
½ oz./15 g. cream of tartar	½ oz. cream of tartar
3 quarts/3½ litres boiling water	15 cups (7½ pints) boiling water
1 oz./25 g. fresh yeast	1 cake compressed yeast
1 slice toast	1 slice toast

Pare off the yellow part of lemon rind and squeeze juice into a bowl, add sugar, ginger and cream of tartar. Pour the boiling water over. When lukewarm add the yeast, creamed with a little of the beer and spread on the toast. Ferment for 24 hours, then skim, strain, bottle and tie down securely.

The beer will be ready to drink in 3 days.

Cider

Cider is the pure juice of the apples, squeezed out with a press so that the pips as well as the pulp are crushed, releasing the aromatic flavour. The southern counties of England have their own special cider apples, each claiming to have the best, and when every fruit-grower had his own cider press, rivalry was keen. The juice of the crushed apples ran out into a stone trough where it stayed until the sediment sunk and bubbles rose to the surface. Cider is never strained; it is poured through a hole in the trough, and, to get it clear, it must stand undisturbed until a test shows that it is clear enough to bottle.

A good cider can be made without a press, crushing the apples with a mallet in an old stone sink raised from the ground, so that the juice can run out of the drain-hole into a tub. When the sediment has sunk, and the surface is covered with bubbles, the juice should be drawn off into a cask, the bung lightly put in, and the cider left undisturbed to work. Only practice and experience can tell you when it is 'working' properly; old hands can tell by listening to the cider 'singing' in the cask.

If sparkling cider is wanted, it must be bottled before fermentation ceases, but the corks must be firmly wired down.

Perry

Perry is made from pears by the same process as Cider.

Index